DISRUPT OR DIE

An Educator's Journey

CAROL CAMPBELL-FULLARD

ISBN: 979-8-218-01368-4

PRINTED AND BOUND IN THE UNITED STATES OF AMERICA

DEDICATION

This story chronicles a personal journey and its connection to my roles and experiences in education as a teacher, assistant principal, and principal.

This book is dedicated to LOVE!

Love of God

Love of Self

Love of my Family

Love of Friends

Love of Students

Love of Education

Love of truth that seeks to Heal!

LOVE

TABLE OF CONTENTS

BREAKFAST

Mornings signal a fresh start. It's the first part of our day that brings forth new opportunities. This renewed moment frees us from the darkness of night. It is the hope and promise of a new beginning. Mornings give us a peek into the blossoming moments of each day's transformation. It is our right to start again, dismissing yesterday's anguish, pain, and frustration. The new light of day illuminates a path for each person to rise again and embrace a new promise in its freshest and most poignant form.

With time I've learned to love the streams of light that peek through the sky to bring the morning's hope. It is my moment of peace and happiness. It is my moment of gratitude. It is my moment to begin again. It is my moment to wake up in love with myself and the world that surrounds me.

I watched as a steady stream of bodies walked through the front door. There were smiling faces, grimaces, the sounds of laughter, and a variety of unassuming looks crossing the threshold of our school building. I always paid close attention to everyone in order to assess which adult or student was having a good or bad day. I spent time examining body language and noticing those who walked in a hurried fashion and those who dragged themselves with every step they took. There were those who walked with their heads up and others who studied the floor with each step, never wanting to make eye contact. The elusive and passing glance of someone could easily communicate and set the tone of a school day. It was important to be super observant every morning. Inside these school walls lie the dreams, hopes, and burdens of adults and children. As a principal, I have been tasked with observing, managing, and addressing everyone the minute they enter the building.

As the sounds of hurried feet made their way through the halls to varied destinations, it's always the goal of an administrator to control the narrative. There may be lots of movement going on around me, but I am focused on voices that may be too loud, the white noise coupled with hurried motions of too many children headed in one direction. That usually meant one thing–FIGHT! My goal each morning was to sweep all those sounds safely into classrooms without incident. Once they were positioned in their seats, each day, we planted the airwaves with our daily seeds of affirmation. It was an invitation to new opportunities. It was a pledge of hope, excellence, and pride.

"Excellence is mandatory.
Therefore, I will give my best every day!
With faith, focus, and follow-through, I can achieve anything…"

As you begin reading this journey, I encourage you to take time each day to affirm and embrace the dawning of a new day. Moreover, eagerly champion the greatness that lives within because it holds the gallant spirit of aspiration and perseverance. Today, take some time to reflect and write your own affirmation.

"Today I am ….

HOMEROOM

ESSENTIAL QUESTION: *Where do our stories begin?*

She was active, a go-getter in every sense of the word. I admired her work ethic and complete enthusiasm. She was a straight "A" student active in student government. She always seemed to be a part of some type of planning committee trying to make the school a better place. Always one of the first students at school and many times the last one to leave. I admired her tenacity and vigor for life. She was going to grow up and do great things.

One day as I was getting ready to leave school, I noticed her sitting out front at the school's security desk. "Taylor, why are you still here?"

"I don't know. I'm not ready to go home yet, she mumbled."

"Girl! I need you to go home before your mother sends out a search party!" I joked.

"She don't care!" I heard her ramble.

"Don't say that!" I urged.

"You don't understand, Ms. Fullard."

"What don't I understand?"

"Nothing. I don't want to talk about it." She began to gather her things, and we walked out the door together. There was a lingering silence between us.

"Taylor, if you ever need to talk, I'm here!"

"Thanks. I'm good." And with that, she scurried across the street to go home. I got in my car and thought about Taylor on the drive home. There was something that overshadowed the light-hearted young girl I was used to seeing. For the first time, I saw a sadness in her eyes I'd never seen before.

The next day as I went to open the school doors, Taylor was the first one standing there. She plastered a smile on her face and greeted me with a Good Morning. However, I looked past the smile to see the same sadness. I wrestled with my thoughts and wondered if I had missed this all along?

"How are you?"

"Good! And you?"

"Fine, thank you. Enjoy breakfast!" She smiled and hustled to the cafeteria for breakfast. I walked away from our exchange, donning a smile as I masked the concern that lingered in the back of my mind. I continued to greet students but still thought about Taylor. The day ended and I never crossed paths with her again. I was making my way around the building to check on the after-school programs but never found her. As I entered the main office to gather my things to leave, I spotted Taylor out of the corner of my eye. "What are you doing here?" I practically sang!

"I want to talk to you about something." She whispered. At that moment, I knew she was ready to pour out her heart. We walked into my office, sat at the table near the Kleenex and Taylor began to spill.

"I don't want to go home," She cried.

"Why? What's going on?"

"My mom hasn't really been coming home?"

"What do you mean?"

"My mother drinks, and sometimes she doesn't always come home. I'm just tired of it! She was doing okay but then started drinking again. I have been living with this all my life and I can't do it anymore! When my sister was there, it was easier, but she moved out. I think she's doing drugs again too. Why can't she stop and just be my mother? I just don't understand why she can't stop?"

Her tears began to overflow, and once again, in that instant, I am reminded of the trauma-filled children I serve. There are never any "right words." There are only words that fill spaces and time to ease them through a journey they didn't plan and a passage they must endure to get to the next stage of their life. These are the faces I see that bear no fault but shoulder the blame. I am reminded of my own family hurts as I think of the right words to tell her as she experiences the betrayal of a loved one. How do I distance myself to speak words of comfort without revealing my own childhood despair? The difference between us would be her display of bravery as she shared her pain, and today, it wouldn't fall on deaf ears. I picked up the phone that day and made two calls. It was my attempt at confronting the perpetrator and finding Taylor the support she needed to confront and heal a pain that she did not cause but had to endure. Today I would give her the opportunity to talk and tell the narrative aloud that consumed the spaces in her life so she could begin to grieve and heal. It would be another late night at school seeking to repair and restore the emotional upheaval of a child.

✳ ✳ ✳ ✳ ✳

Tired from my walk, I decided to sit in the park and watch the children play. One little girl caught my eye as she seemed so daring and wanted to play on everything. Her smile lit up each time she went high on the swing. Her smile and laugh were so contagious that I found myself grinning while watching her yell, "Daddy, push the swing higher!" As I looked past her to the clouds hovering over the playground, I began to think about my childhood and wondered when the laughter stopped for me. When and how did I learn to master being happy even though on the inside I was screaming?

I got up from the bench, thinking about what needed to be done next. I aimlessly walked to my car with tears filling my eyes, blurry, straining to hold back what was inevitably meant to happen. And with one blink, streams of water began to flow down my face dampening my cheeks and exposing my pain. I couldn't stop them. Each wipe only brought more tears to rapidly cascade down my face. I could feel beads of tears caressing my neck and disappearing into my shirt collar. I hurried inside the car and suddenly felt the need to belt out in a loud voice all the pain that had been hurting me for years. I didn't care if others heard as they passed. I needed to release this pain, it was 50 years overdue. The hums of the ignition and the sounds of the engine lulled me into a guttural cry as I screamed, "Why?" My hands began flailing in anger, punching the steering wheel and dashboard in front of me. "Why me?" I yelled as a person expecting a response, but there was none!

The five-minute ride to my house on that day took about an hour. I drove up and down the strip of highway near the house to clear my mind and organize my thoughts. All this time, these thoughts had been buried so deep and just like that, in the flash of a little girl's laughter and a call for her dad, everything came rushing back. The memories were so vivid. It was as if they had been longing for permission to surface and reveal themselves, yearning for healing, resolution, and closure. I had just stumbled into a dance of discovery that required me to heal a pain I didn't want to remember.

I carefully careened the car into the driveway with the sounds of Frankie Beverly and Maze playing in the background. I sat there, letting the soulful music pulse through my body as they crooned in a harmonizing voice, *"We are one. Our love will see us through."* At that very moment, my body released some of its tension. I let the song finish playing and looked up to see my husband open the front door. I didn't let his gesture dissuade my thoughts or provoke me to move towards the door and enter the house. I continued sitting in the car, wiping my face, and tracing my breath as I inhaled and exhaled with sounds of music loudly swirling around my car. I could see him peering out, but just as quickly as he appeared, he disappeared in the same manner, leaving the door open for me to enter when I was ready.

As the song shifted into *Happy Feelings*, I turned the car off and went inside. I walked directly into the family room to speak with my husband. He glanced up at me, remote in hand, and before I could say hello. He uttered, "What's wrong?" I felt my body become uncomfortable and shaky again. I moved to a couch on the other side of the room, imploring my mouth to open and speak to this man who had a puzzled but worried expression on his face.

"What's wrong? I heard him stammer with concern. "I just have some things I need to figure out right now." I could see the questioning look in his eyes. I quickly mumbled, "I need to sort out some things about my past." As the words flowed out, I forced down my tears from resurfacing again.

In my heart, I just wanted to go and lean into him and cry myself into freedom. Freedom from the pain that was plaguing me. Freedom from this muteness that had been lodged in the depths of my soul. I could see his helpless expression as if he was still wondering if my behavior had anything to do with our marriage.

I spoke up to ease the look on his face and just repeated, "I am just remembering some things from my past that I had forgotten happened to me."

"What brought this on? He questioned.

I loosely shared the story about the little girl on the swing and how when she called out for her dad, I remembered needing my dad at a critical time and he was not there to protect me, keep me safe. I would spend the rest of my life needing my dad that way but never really connecting and having that void filled. Instead, my dad and I would go through years of strained conversations and unresolved issues until about a year before he died. Only then would we finally face and grapple with the history of our tattered relationship to bring a level of overdue restoration to our lives.

Unfortunately, even in the face of our resolution, he would die, never really knowing the pain I endured at the hands of others. I could never bring myself to tell him how the dreams of a little girl were shattered by her closest relatives. He would walk me down the aisle for my wedding but never really knew that his little girl would never be able to truly love fully out without expecting the sharp and stinging pain of hurt and betrayal to accompany it. He would never know that my experiences as a child, coupled with the rocky relationship of a "father and daughter," would lay the foundation for how I would love. I would flirt with relationships that had minimal expectations or remain loyal to a veneer definition of love. The depths of love would not change for me until I had my first child, and even then, it would never fill the deep void of a father's love I knew was there but could not feel.

I looked at my husband and began whispering parts of my story choking on the words as they left my mouth, "I was sexually abused as a child by someone close to me." Before he could respond, I quivered in a low but steady voice, "That's all I want to say for now. I need more processing time." I got up from the couch and left the room. At that moment, I repeated the same actions I had been doing all my life. I was trying to put the thought away–to escape from the feelings and neatly compartmentalize them as if they would go away on their own. This time was different. As I fell on the bed in my room, the tears kept coming, and the pain would not subside to another place. This time my past pain had slapped me in the face and beckoned me to bear the emotional bruises of my five-year-old self that came flooding back.

I was so excited about putting on my pretty new dress. I put on my favorite shoes to match my new dress and couldn't wait to take pictures. I remembered how the bottom of my dress would sway wide while I spun. The print on the fabric had my favorite colors, purple and white. The ruffles gathered around my neck and were also tapered at the trim of my sleeves. My socks perfectly matched the top of my dress as it ruffled around my ankle. Finally, it was time to take pictures!

I stood in front of the photographer and gave him my best smile. I felt like a model and loved how the sharp, clear sounds from the camera signaled the opportunity to impersonate a different pose.

When the camera stopped, GG walked over to me in a matter-of-fact tone and said, "Remove your clothes."

"Okay, I mumbled," secretly sad that we were done taking pictures.

As I turned to walk away, I heard her say, "Where are you going? Take off your clothes right here!"

I was confused. What did she mean? A strange man standing with a camera less than three feet away would see me getting undressed. My eyes must have revealed the confusion because I heard her follow up with, "We're going to take some pictures of you without clothes."

I gasped, "Why?" and could feel the tears immediately rolling down my face at a mad and hurried pace. I squealed, "I don't want to take off my clothes."

This time a stern, steady, but booming voice bellowed, "Take off your clothes now! Don't let me have to tell you again."

With each article of clothing I removed, the more the tears came down, overpowering my face and blurring my sight.

"What are you crying about? Move your hands! Don't let me tell you again to move your hands!" The voices loomed overhead like dark shadows swallowing me up.

I was scared. My objections went unheard. With each click of the camera, I cried, embracing the tormenting and frightening pain running up and down my body. I crouched, willing myself to shrink. My small hands kept moving to cover up the exposed parts in an attempt to limit my exposure. Nothing was working.

"Stand up straight," GG said sternly. The demands became more aggressive and louder, "Stand up straight and move your hands!"

I could hear the whispers of a man's voice, "It's okay. Just smile at me! Give me a big smile!"

I stood there confused and wondered why he would tell me that? I'm not having fun. Couldn't they see the terror in my eyes and tears streaming down my face? I kept looking at GG, begging her with my voice, body language, and tears to make this stop. Why was she letting this man take nude pictures of me? Somewhere in my 5-year-old mind, I knew this was wrong. Anything that gave me this much pain had to be wrong. I wasn't strong enough to fight back. The tears continued to stream - a steady flow of pain, anger, and helplessness covering my face. I'm not sure how long we took pictures. I think my unwillingness to cooperate took longer than I spent taking pictures. I'm not sure how and why it stopped. Did GG finally understand and see the fear in my eyes? Did she feel a sense of guilt for making me do this? Years later, I would come across one of those pictures and wonder where the rest of them ended up.

That picture shoot may have taken 10, 15, or even 20 minutes; I don't really remember. However, the scattered memories gleaned from that moment impacted the rest of my life. It laid the foundation for my insecurities, anger, and pain. It was the hurt that never healed. It was the pain I buried beneath molestation, betrayal, and infidelity. It was the bitter taste I shared in words to diminish others. It was the seed that brought forth the fruit of depression, negative self-worth, and thoughts of suicide. It was a seed that had been buried so many years ago that I forgot it existed and although it had been manifesting throughout my whole life. How could I heal a *pain* I couldn't remember?

For years I had filed away the pain of my childhood. There were glimpses that surfaced, but for the most part, it was buried six feet into the depths of my mind. This time around was different, the memories came up and lingered. It was looming just below the surface, waiting to be acknowledged, healed, and reconciled. It was a piece of my life that needed to be embraced as the anchor of my experiences. This was a piece of the puzzle that I wanted to misplace in a box of lost and unwanted souvenirs.

My release would come as I began to pen my voice and truth into written words. It was clear that unmuting myself was the journey to restoration. It was time to share the feelings from deep within my soul to begin carving a life that no longer ached and felt stuck wandering around looking for the safety of a dad. I had finally found protection from a father that would heal the hurt and supply all my needs. I had treated God all these years like a safety, the last line of defense. However, I could clearly see all this time he has been my deepest defender up front and ready to provide support for anything I would run up against. He was keeping me together all this time, waiting patiently for the pilgrimage of his purpose to come to fruition in my life.

I sat in the living room comfy in my self-care corner, enjoying the carefully brewed lemon ginger tea, contemplating the words that rang out from the morning's devotion. Today was a little heavier than usual as I thought about my two daughters. It was time for me to tell them my story. It was time to be a transparent reflection of what I hoped they would do for their children one day. I needed to display the bravery and courage I preached to them all their lives. The uneasiness of it felt like a lump stuck in my throat -strained and obstructed from the contents of my traumatic memories.

After carefully arranging words and thoughts in my head, I called my youngest daughter to me so the conversation could begin. As we sat at the dining room table, my hands glossed over the phone and laptop keys as if looking for a comforting nudge and a reassuring caress. As I looked over at her, I could see the gaze of curiosity probing my face searching for answers even before one word had been uttered.

With an anxious yet soft tone, I said, "There are some things you need to know about my childhood."

"Like What?" she said in a quizzical tone.

"As a child, I was sexually abused by someone close to me."

"What do you mean, mommy?"

"Someone I trusted hurt me." As I began to tell the story of GG, my heart was filled with anguish as I saw the sadness and pain my daughter's face revealed to me. She couldn't understand why anyone would do that to a 5-year-old. In my head and heart, I prayed she would never share a full comprehension of this agony residing in me. Like so many others, this story would be a lesson about trust, family, and the lines that should never be crossed. More importantly, I needed her to know the power of her voice. "Your voice is your power! Don't let anyone ever try to keep you quiet if they've hurt or violated you. Don't be afraid to tell your truth. Don't suffer in silence. Tell someone!"

"Why didn't you tell someone?"

"I was scared and didn't know what would happen to me." My daughter hugged me, and we didn't need to speak another word. She felt my pain. She heard my words. My only hope now was that she would walk in the advice of never hoarding or hiding any pain that might come her way.

I made a few calls and sent some texts to my older daughter, but it seemed like she was avoiding the conversation. I was sure to point out in my messages that it was about my childhood, but still, the response was tepid at best. I finally took a step back and realized this was my "feeling" child. She had already known some of my history and probably was uneasy or nervous about learning more bad things. Unfortunately, she had learned all too well how to bury her unresolved feelings and pain too. It has long been the guilt I have shouldered while raising her early on as a single parent. We were always in motion and on a perpetual cycle of survival. She too, would come to experience the void of consistency in a father-daughter relationship that would impact her interactions for years to come.

As the FaceTime call connected, I ushered in polite conversation to create a space of comfort. When a moment of silence interrupted, I shared my story. "Who did this to you?" she quipped angrily.

"I'd rather not say. I just want you to know my story."

"Mom, let me know so we can take care of them." As she angrily tossed the words, I could see the hurt she felt for me. Just then, I saw myself. I saw that fighting spirit that had been angry with the world. That attitude of *don't start nothing, won't be nothing* was written all over her. I had been looking at my reflection through her. Growing I didn't experience permission to share my pain and its progressive grip on my life. Back then, my parents were so caught up in the discomforts of their marriage that I chose to withdraw into the weight of my burden. Little did I know, the load would only get heavier.

FIRST PERIOD

ESSENTIAL QUESTION: *How do we survive adversity caused by familial love?*

The day was long, and my tiredness seemed to sink into the wooden chair as I rested my body. I began to aimlessly shuffle the papers on my desk when a light rap came across my door as one of my favorite students, Arlene, walked inside the classroom. "Hey Girl, why are you still here?" I said in a matter-of-fact tone, still straightening up my desk.

"I don't know, she whispered." By the tone of her voice, I could tell something wasn't right.

"What's wrong?" I uttered only to see her eyes filled with tears.

"I don't want to go home," she cried as the tears began to flow in heavy succession.

"Why? What happened?"

"My mother doesn't want me!"

"What are you talking about?"

"I think she hates me. I remind her of bad things!" I was confused and bewildered about what she was saying. I dug in my desk drawer and pulled out a napkin so she could wipe her face. I waited for her to clean herself up some and then asked what she meant.

"My mother was raped by someone, and then she had me!" I was stunned and watched as the tears really began to flow. My heart leaped in connection with her pain. I hugged her around the shoulder as she wept as I searched in my mind about what to say next. This was only my second year as a teacher, and to say that most of my education had become on-the-job training was putting it mildly. There was not one class I took that gave training on how to deal with this topic! There was the child abuse and neglect training, but this was a new one for me! As the tears and her heavy breathing slowed, I asked, "Why do you think she hates you? Did she say something to you?"

"No, but I can tell. She treats me differently from my brother!"

"I'm always getting in trouble and it's the way she looks at me!" At this moment, there was such a connection that developed between us. She would never understand how my heart ached for both her and her mother. The strength it must have taken to live your life every day, remembering that this beautiful creature you produced came from a consecration of hate and violence to your body. How does one reconcile love with the vision of a child you didn't give permission to conceive. This girl looks to me for answers, and little does she know I have spent a lifetime looking for my own answers. How do I tell her that her mother is trying to heal through a pain that she is a constant reminder of? How do I tell her I know similar scars in a different space and time? How does she learn to heal from her mother's wound?

✳ ✳ ✳ ✳ ✳

I remember standing in the airport, fascinated by the people coming and going, watching as people screamed, hugged, and kissed at the sight of their loved ones. There was a blanket of happiness all around us. Their infectious euphoria made me happy and excited to finally meet Mark, my uncle from Jamaica. I heard so many stories and couldn't wait to see him in the flesh. I stood there in between my mother and father. My mother looked eager but happy, and dad just looked blank, no hint of emotion escaped his face. Finally, I saw my mother waving her hand feverishly and heard her yelling, "Mark! Mark! I'm over here!" I peeked around her to see the figure of a young man coming my way. He embraced my mother and shook dad's hands. Then he looked at me and said, "Carol! My niece! Carol!" I smiled as he gave me a great big hug. Once in the car, I remembered falling asleep on his arm on the way home. I remembered thinking that having Uncle Mark around would be great!

My family home had long served as the place where people sometimes came if they needed a place to stay. There was my dad's friend, Bosey, and my Uncle Frank. I guess having someone take over the other room in our home helped put more money on the table. I can remember the bass seeping through the speakers as Bob Marley wailed, the voices of laughter that cried out to a joke, the clap of Dominoes as they hit the table, and the promising smell of food wafting through the hallway and rooms of our apartment. These moments in my house were special yet too far apart. At this very moment, I would forget the shouts of angry parents or the silent lulls of frustration that often took up residence in this place I called home. I was able to escape accusatory arguments that circled around infidelity, finances, and raising children. This was the home I loved. The home that entertained friends and hosted family gatherings. Eventually, that home would just become a house full of tension and resentment.

His footsteps jarred me out of my sleep. I heard him whisper, "Can I lay down here on your bed?" I could see the outline of his face in the dark as he rubbed his head in a tired fashion.

"Yes," I grumbled in a sleepy voice and turned over to curl in a fetal position. As the slumber of sleep began to sink in, I could feel his arms reach over and bring me close to him. I kept my eyes closed and welcomed the protection until I felt his lips pressing against my neck, kissing me. I began to move, but he held me tight, climbing on top of me, asking if it was okay, but pressing forward without waiting for a response. I laid still as he continued to kiss me and forge ahead to enter me. I was so oblivious and didn't understand that at age nine, this shouldn't be happening to me. As he reached down to complete his journey, I remember pushing him really hard off of me and yelling, "you're wetting me," and running to the bathroom. I cleaned myself off, confused and shaken about what had happened. I sat down on the cold porcelain floor tracing the shapes with my fingers and inspecting the black and white color patterns. I didn't want to go back to that room. I'm not sure how much time went by before I got up to leave the comfort of our bathroom. I slowly entered the room to see he had left. I could hear echoes of him shifting on the couch, and my heart released a gasp of relief. I entered my room and closed the door. Sleep was hard to grasp that night. My eyes stayed until daylight crept in to alert me of a new day. My memories of the next day have always remained a fuzzy haze, unable to remember how I behaved, spoke, or interacted with others. It was clear that I had buried this incident just like I did the others that happened in my lifetime, an inappropriate touch or unwanted kiss.

As years rolled by and life at home changed to a single-family household, so did my friendly and forgiving demeanor. I became a different little girl on the inside. I wasn't afraid to fight. It didn't make a difference if you were a boy or girl. I was always willing to scrap. I never let another person take advantage of me, insult me or just plain dare tell me that I couldn't or wouldn't do anything about the problem. I had become angry and bitter. I hung onto a deep hate that would carve out how I dealt with relationships and led my life.

Years later, as I struggled through the illness of a mother, I would receive an unexpected knock on my door. It was Uncle Mark offering his help and support. I was initially rattled by his presence. I let him in the house and used the door as my shield to avoid his stirring greetings that required an embrace. I closed the door and scurried around his frame to create distance between us. He gave me a quizzical look and stammered, "I don't get a hug?"

"I'm good."

"Okay," he retorted in an annoying tone.

"I was just coming by to check on you. Your mother is very worried about you. She's concerned that you might need help with the bills. I came by to see if you need any help. Do you need any money?"

"No." I purposely kept my responses short and to the point. I wanted him to get the hell out of my house!

"Are you sure? I'm here to help!" At that moment, a shift occurred in me, and a flood of words coupled with restrained emotions was released.

"I don't need anything from you. I am fine. I don't want your help at all. You don't think I remember what you did to me as a child?"

"What are you talking about?" I could feel my anger boiling, but I stayed the course of stern and controlled reproach.

"I remember that you molested me as a child!"

"No, you must be mistaken." In that instant, our eyes became locked, and I hurled a gaze of despise that sought to permeate his countenance and soul. It must have worked because before I knew it, he had blubbered out a weak apology and an offer to help me if I needed it. My gaze continued as I asked him to leave. Our paths would not cross again until decades later upon the death of my grandmother and then again at the funeral of his son.

SECOND PERIOD

ESSENTIAL QUESTION: *What is The Seamless Gap Between Death and Birth?*

"I need to see the principal! I need to talk to her now!" I heard the elevated voice of what could only be a demanding parent. I could hear the stress and frustration that accompanied the request. My heart began a slow race, bracing myself for the conversation that was about to take place. I did an immediate prep of mindset to ensure that the conversation would be a positive one. I emerged from my office, still feeling uncertain and anxious while meticulously planning the next steps.

"Good Morning. Did you need to see me? I said calmly."

"Yes! I need to talk to you! I'm tired of all these calls I keep getting for every little thing!"

"Okay, please give me five minutes to finish up something and we can meet."

"Okay. Enough is enough!"

I went back to the office, closed the door, went to my desk, pulled open the drawer and began to read my devotion. I knew this conversation needed to have God at the wheel, so I said nothing that would make the parent even more enraged. I read, prayed and sat in the stillness of the quietness to gather my thoughts and listen for direction. I went a little over the five minutes as disclosed because it was important for me to get this conversation right. Finally, I arose from my desk feeling settled and confident to hear the issues and put out the fire. In a low but earnest voice, I murmured, "This is what I do!" I opened the door and began. "Ms. Johnson, please come back." I motioned. As she walked toward me, I could see the anger, frustration, and something else that really held my attention, FEAR. I trailed behind her and eventually eased behind my desk to sit down.

"How can I help you today?" I questioned in a very calm voice. And before I could get the words completely out a flow of thoughts came pouring out of her mouth swirled in a roughness and hostility that would leave most people gasping and speechless. But, I was ready and knew my parents. This was her passion and fear cascading onto my desk and echoing off the walls in my office. It was raw yet compelling and exhibited the insecurities and fears of a mother. At that moment, I was not just an administrator, I was a mother too! I listened to her complaints and addressed them collectively.

"I hear your concern and know you want the best for Reginald. He is a very bright young man and has the ability to do great things. I have been in classes with him where he is personable and his intelligence shines. I have also stepped into rooms where he has cursed at the teacher or administrator and has taken a long time to calm down! Can you tell me how we can reach him so he is successful?" I'll never know what shifted her mood. Was it my question? Was it the compliments about her son? Was it the calmness of my voice?

At that moment, the anger turned to a flood of tears as she began to share her struggles raising Reginald. "I have tried everything, but he doesn't listen unless I'm threatening to beat him. I put him in football so he can have positive males around him and it will work for a minute and then he's right back to getting in trouble. I don't know what to do anymore. I'm so tired and don't think I can do this anymore. I just want to kill myself and end it all. I just need some peace." As the words of self-harm emerged from her mouth, I could sense the anguish, see the agony and understand those feelings of weariness and shame that secretly taunt a person's mind full of discouragement–urging them to give up. However, no one would be quitting on life today. Not on my watch! As I shuffled the tissue across my desk, I reminded her of the strength she had as a mother, the new baby that needed her to live and the difference that was being made every day she fought to stay alive. Her brokenness was evident as she agreed to let me connect her with outside services and resources. And as we spent the next four hours together, our relationship changed from a parent-administrator connection to mothers on a journey to find healing and self-care. I didn't do informal observations that day or visit many classrooms, but I did help save a life.

Several months later, that parent would be gunned down in the most tragic way as the unintended victim protecting someone she loved. She would leave behind children that grieve her loss and have to find a new beginning somewhere else. Although I would never understand the pain of losing a parent to such violence, I intimately understood the aching pain of losing a mother.

✳ ✳ ✳ ✳ ✳

I sat nestled on the living room couch, watching my mother pack for her trip. She was so excited to be going home! It had been a long time since she traveled to Jamaica, and as the Admiral Bailey song goes, *"When me check it out, Lord, Nowhere no better than yard!"* I listened to her quiz me several times about locking the door, inviting company over and, most importantly, using the stove responsibly. I hemmed and hawed while giggling to exasperate her as she tried to be serious. As excited as she was about going away, I was equally as excited about staying home by myself! Little did I know that this first Christmas apart would foreshadow many more to come.

Regardless of the time we would spend apart, there is one tradition that remained, decorating the Christmas tree together. We always did it late and disagreed on the decorations as she always brought out too many colors to put on the tree with the electronic bird, she hid in the branches that made sharp, high-pitched chattering noises. I loathed it, but she relished in the sounds it made. I observed her eagerness and enthusiasm to decorate the tree and knew this was important to her. Somehow it seemed to fill a personal void. It was a reflection of the family time we rarely got to spend together because she was always working to make ends meet. Even though I graduated from college and now had a job, she wouldn't take my money. She used to say, "save that little bit of money you're making." She definitely was not exaggerating! My salary was awful! I loved my job but hated the salary. As we continued working on the tree, I could see the tiredness frame her face. I knew she needed this vacation. I knew she needed rest. Although she no longer worked two jobs, it wasn't unusual for her to pick up another shift if needed. It was at that moment that I reached out, put my arms around her shoulder and volunteered to finish the tree. I will be forever grateful for that moment and the many others like it because they would be few and far between.

There was a muffled sound coming from the bathroom. I carefully walked down the hallway to investigate. "Mom, are you okay?" Initially, there was no response and I began to panic.

"Mom! Is everything okay?"

The door opened slightly and I heard her whisper, "I think I need to go to the doctor."

"Why? I said nervously. Did you hurt yourself?" She shook her head no and beckoned for me to come over. What I saw next paralyzed me with fear. The bowl was full of blood and clots. Since she had a hysterectomy years before, I knew it couldn't be that time of the month.

"Mom, what's going on? Do I need to call an ambulance?" I cried. Instantly, I looked at her face and realized my hysterics were not helping the situation. Instead, I lowered my voice and asked the same question again.

"No, I want to go to my doctor. Please call him so we can go today." She directed me to her personal phone book, and I found the number. The offices weren't open yet, but I felt compelled to restlessly sit by the phone, waiting for the clock to hit 9:00 am. As she came into the room, I could see the fear in her eyes. My mom had always been a fighter. It felt like she was the strongest woman I knew. However, all of a sudden, without warning, my mother had changed before my eyes. That strength had been erased by a look of fear.

She was scared and unsure. Her energy was low, not robust like I had become accustomed to. At that very moment, I knew we had switched roles. It was my time to be strong and unalarming. It was my time to bear our load and make us safe again. It was my time to step into the woman she had been raising me to be all these years. It was my time! The words were few and at times, the silence seemed deafening as we both listened to ticks from the clock, desiring the time to strike 9:00 am already. As the numbers from the digital clock finally changed, I rushed to make the call. I think the secretary heard the fear in my voice as I asked to be seen on the same day. She obliged and gave us an appointment.

This moment was so strange for me. I could feel myself taking over and immediately managing my mom. I went into the closet and picked out something comfortable and easy to wear. I combed her hair and encouraged her to eat, but she settled for tea instead. As she sipped her tea in slow motion, I called the cab and watched her hands shake with worry. I held in my feelings and trembled on the inside and wondered what was going to become of us!

The cab ride was silent. I looked out the window at the busy streets, watching people move on with their daily lives as mine felt like it was at a standstill. I reached over to hold my mother's warm and sweaty hands. She squeezed my hands and forced a smile to reassure me. I flashed a grin back at her, swallowing the nerves that I felt coming up to choke me. We entered the doctor's office, still holding on to the silence and fear that seemed to be binding us. As we both aimlessly looked through the magazines around us, time stood still as we waited for her name to be called. I gasped as they called her back. Immediately, I began to pray.

After what felt like a long time, she emerged from the back with a bunch of papers in her hands. I got up and we walked outside. "Mom, what did he say?"

"He wants me to get some lab work done and come back to him."

"When?"

"Now. Their offices are down the street." The wind whipped across my face as we walked in a hurried fashion to the lab place. I could see the trees sway with passion back and forth. It was another moment of silent transportation. I was frustrated and wanted to know more but didn't push it. I kept whispering to myself, *Keep calm; it's going to be okay. She'll tell you more when it's time.*

The office had an antiseptic and stale smell that made me want to puke. The hallway light was really dim and my discomfort grew even more. As we sat in the hard chairs, I heard my mother say, "It's going to be alright. They are just going to run some tests and then the doctor will know what to do." We were there for a very long time. I walked in and out of their offices just to feel the cold breeze across my face. I needed air. I needed to know what was going on! I needed more than anyone could give me at that moment. After what seemed like hours, she was done and we took a taxi back home to play the awful game of waiting.

"Cancer. The doctor said I have cancer. They want to operate as soon as possible to try and remove it. I am having surgery next week. It will be at..." The words began to fade into oblivion. Everything sounded like a distant echo as her words hurled out one after another. The only word I could hear was CANCER. I looked up to see her hopeful smile and knew I couldn't cry! Somewhere inside of me, I knew that this moment couldn't be about me, so I did what became normal-suffer in silence so she could be her brave self. I suffered in silence so she could appear in control and confident. I suffered in silence as they rolled her bed down the hall to take her into surgery. I suffered in silence as they opened and closed her up five days later and said there was nothing they could do! I suffered in silence when they told me she only had three months to live. I suffered in silence.

Months of running to doctors, emergency rooms, and hospital visits would dominate every area of my life. I would sleep on hard chairs in waiting areas and hospital rooms. I would cry to my best friends and boyfriend, but put on the bravest face in front of her. I joked, laughed, sang and would give her the latest gossip! I tried anything to take her mind off the tubes that often clothed her body. It was our new normal.

The summer edged its way into my life as I struggled to remember the fanfare of spring. I grappled with remembering when the flowers came into bloom and when the echoes of birds began to chirp everywhere. All I could seem to remember from spring was the rain. The heaviness of thunderstorms penetrated every aspect of my life. The daily deluge of showers was constantly beating against the windows of my life, trapping me to operate in an emotionless state. This was my formal introduction to grief, an uninvited guest, dismantling my life and leaving a lifetime of destruction behind.

Taking care of the bills also became my new normal. It became time to change jobs and with encouragement from two friends, I decided to apply for a teaching job. I modeled my new outfit in front of my mother. She gave me the thumbs up. "You look good!" she yelled. With my purse and portfolio in hand, I was off to my job interview to become an English teacher. I kept thinking to myself, what am I doing? I never wanted to be a teacher! But, with mommy being sick, I had to get a better-paying job to help with the bills. Plus, if it didn't work out, I had the summer off with pay to look for a new job. I entered the building ready to sell myself even though I had never taught a day in my life. However, I did get along well with teenagers and my minor was writing in college. I stepped into the principal's office and 45 minutes later, I was hired on the spot to be a 7th Grade English teacher, provided all my paperwork got submitted to the board and was approved.

I couldn't wait to get home and tell her the good news! In my own way, I was hoping that this happy moment would just be the fix we needed to get back to our old lives. She had the biggest smile on her face, and it stretched from ear to ear. "I knew you would get it!" she laughed. "I am so proud of you!" Something was different about her. There was a peace in her voice as she said, "I'm so proud you have your car and a new job!" I knew this accomplishment mattered. It was just like graduating college. My mother was proud that her little girl had beat the odds that are usually framed for a girl growing up in the Bronx, the poorest borough in New York City.

Three months had come and gone, and she was still around! I remember the joy felt each day. It will always be etched in my mind, the laughter and smiles of once again beating the odds. The summer edged its way into our lives with a whirlwind of ups and downs, cries, and laughter. Everywhere I looked, family and friends came to support us and even though she ended up in the hospital, things began to take a turn for the better. One evening we sat in her room laughing and joking. My cousin, godmother, and I were doing our best to make the laughter flow. Eventually my grandmother showed up food in hand. It was as if my mom was a kid again, smiling with anticipation as Momma unveiled the homemade chicken soup she requested. She sipped her soup and beamed with excitement as she told us her brother was on his way from Canada to see her! A continuous grin plastered her face that evening as she told me to go out with my friends. "You're always here. Go out!" she lovingly scolded.

My Godmother agreed to stay at the hospital with her that night. I was elated because she was getting better and everyone could see and feel it. Her spirited demeanor had returned in a dynamic way. I left the hospital that night with a renewed spirit. Cancer had not beaten us. We had beaten it. My mother would spend years telling people about her miraculous recovery and the power of God. I was experiencing a sense of peace that had escaped me for the last seven months. There was a shift of relief and gratitude as we appeared to be moving away from the pain and suffering.

That night I went out with my friends to enjoy the sounds of reggae, laughter, and the eye candy of men strolling through the place. I had a boyfriend but loved to live vicariously through my friends, who encountered their own share of drama and fun that night. As everyone made their way home, my cousin and I hustled to the apartment and crashed. We woke up a few hours later to gossip about the night and make plans to visit the hospital. As we embroiled ourselves in laughter and all the drama of that night, the phone rang.

"Hello!" I chuckled.

"Carol?"

"Yes. Hey Aunty Cynthia!" I continued to giggle.

"She's gone."

"What do you mean? What are you talking about?"

"She died this morning." I don't remember my next words, just the guttural scream that came from deep inside me. I don't know who took the phone. I remember running into the bathroom and pulling at the shower curtains and falling to feel the coldness of the floor beneath me. There were voices all around me. What were they saying? I didn't know. I didn't *want* to know. I just needed and wanted to see my mother. I had to get to the hospital. I remember the drive. It felt like hours. As we edged up the hill to our destination, I could feel the car careening over to the left in a parking space and didn't understand why we had stopped.

"What are you doing?"

"I'll be right back!" Before I could respond, my boyfriend had disappeared from the car into a store.

"What is he doing?" I yelled. I could feel the hands of my cousin on my shoulder, trying to calm me down. It's okay. He appeared as quickly as he left. Tears began to roll down my eyes again and just then, I knew he too was in pain and trying to delay the obvious. I felt my heart beating heavier as we got closer to the hospital. In my mind, I was screaming for the car to stop and let me out.

We pulled in front of the hospital and without a word, I hopped out of the car and began to run. I could hear voices behind me calling my name, asking me to stop, telling me to wait. I ran down a dimly lit hall, focused on reaching my destination. In my mind, I was hoping there was some type of mistake. I wouldn't believe it until I came face to face with her. As I neared the room, I could hear voices. I saw my Godmother standing there with tears streaming down her face. I looked past her and ran into the room. I stood there looking at the lifeless body wishing we could switch places. I touched her face, hugged her body and kissed her cheek. She didn't respond. She didn't move. I didn't feel the coldness from her body. It just felt still. I touched and pressed, but no response. I could hear people weeping and as I investigated the faces of those in the room it was clear, she was gone. At that moment, an emptiness occupied my heart, never to be filled. In the blink of an eye, there was a seamless transition that occurred from her death to my birth as a woman on my own with no more guidance and expectations from a mother. I felt shattered and alone. Years would go by, and I eventually would get married and even have children of my own. However, the void of a mother's love can never ever be filled–it is an aching pain of eternal loss.

THIRD PERIOD

ESSENTIAL QUESTION: *How does self-love teach others to treat us?*

I peered through my window shades to locate the voices of the students yelling outside. I watched as Camryn yelled, "Where are you going? Where are you going?" I heard a male voice respond, "I'll be back."

She continued yelling, "Deon, where you going?"

"Go inside the building! I'll be back!"

I watched as the anxiety drained from her face and turned to sadness. She quietly entered the building leaving the conversation at the doorway. I left my office and stood in the hallway, ensuring that our paths would cross. As she approached my direction, I put on a big smile and greeted her in an encouraging manner, "Good morning, Camryn!

How are you?"

"Good morning," she uttered less than enthusiastically.

"I like your hair. It's pretty."

She finally smiled, "thank you."

"Have a good day," I replied.

As she walked away, I couldn't help but notice the small round bump that protruded from under her shirt. She was 14 years old and her whole world was about to change. I wondered if she really understood the commitment of being a parent, being a mother, being responsible for another human. In my heart, I knew she didn't really understand how her life was going to change. A young girl pregnant at this age should have surprised me, but that never happened anymore.

That day as I walked around the cafeteria during lunch duty, I made sure to stop by Camryn's table. "Camryn, why aren't you eating?"

"I'm not hungry."

"You can't afford to skip meals. You're eating for two now!"

"I know, but I'm just not hungry."

"Did you eat breakfast today?"

"No."

"Camryn, please know that when you skip meals, the baby suffers. Please try and eat something, even if it's small."

"Okay," she mumbled. We walked over to the lunch line for her to get food.

I glanced over at Camryn's table a few minutes later to see her eating the food with a vengeance.

That afternoon as we dismissed students, I heard the same voices again in the courtyard. "Leave me alone! Leave me alone! You didn't come back like you promised!"

"But, I'm back now!" yelled the same male voice from earlier that day. I watched as Deon put his arms around Camryn. She shrugged away, but he forcefully pulled her back as they walked

off together. Something about that encounter left me uncomfortable. I just hoped my instincts were wrong.

For the next two days, I noticed that Camryn was not in school. We did our attendance calls with no response from her parents. On Friday, she showed up with a small bruise near her temple. I noticed it as she walked in the door and greeted me. I reached out to the school's counselor to find out if she was aware of anything going on. She had heard things but couldn't confirm anything. She even spoke with Camryn, who vehemently denied the rumor. Over the next few weeks, we made it a point to observe her behavior and notice if she came to school with any obvious signs of abuse.

During dismissal one afternoon, I heard two voices yelling. Words of profanity swirled in the hallway. I rushed to see what was going on and saw two students arguing. Although I saw students before me, the argument seemed like that of adults–heavy, grown and full of history. I walked over and Deon exited the building. I escorted Camryn to my office. "Are you okay? I asked. Her eyes filled up with tears and sadness was steep within them. I strained to hear her whisper "yes".

"What's going on?"

"Nothing."

"Why were you talking to each other like that?"

"No reason."

"There's got to be a reason." We sat there in silence.

"Listen, you're about to be a mom and you can't put yourself through that type of stress. It's not good for the baby."

"We just had an argument."

"If he talks to you like that in public, I would hate to hear how he sounds in private."

"He doesn't talk to me like that all the time!"

"He shouldn't talk to you like that anytime!" There was a silence that covered the room again.

"Look, if you have a little girl, it is important that she knows how she should be treated. You're going to have to show her that."

"He don't act like that all the time. He loves me."

"While that may be important. The most important thing is do you love yourself?"

She wiped her face, held down her head and said, "I have to go!"

"Okay. I'm here if you need to talk."

"Okay." And with that, she got up and left my office!

And just like that, I was reminded that true love starts within. It ends up being our compass and road map for how we will let others treat *and* love *us. I have often thought back to that time and wondered where her pain started.*

✳ ✳ ✳ ✳ ✳

Silence filled the house. I woke up early that morning to observe the sun peek through the sky, welcoming me to a new day. As the sun peered through my window, I raised my head and arms to feel its warmth and imagine the reassuring words of a mother's love and inspiration. I was sure she was there with me and that her spirit of love and persistence were flowing through me like a river, ushering me into that new passage of life. I got up and stared in the mirror, looking past my reflection into my soul, but I wasn't ready to confront that part of me. Instead, I brushed my teeth, took a shower, combed my hair and got ready for my first day of teaching, it had been two weeks since I buried the love of my life, my mother.

This new chapter of my life was so bittersweet. I was in a constant battle between depression and elation. All those years of education and no one taught me how to navigate the spaces of heartbreak, anger, disappointment, uncertainty, and unresolved issues. Weeks turned into months and I had learned to put all my emotions on hold for the greater good. While it worked, for the most part, these days I found myself in a daily deluge of feelings or thoughts that were often disconnected and only led to one thing– a bridge of pain that was hard to get over. After a couple of weeks of wandering through this pain, I quickly decided to abort the journey. It was not my time for healing. Just like that, once again, I was burying my pain and withdrawing into the weight of my burden.

Rick Warren says, *"If God is going to do his deepest work in you, it will begin with surrender. So give it all to God; your past regrets, recent problems, your future ambitions, your fears, your dreams, weaknesses, habits, hurts, and hang-ups. Put Christ in the driver's seat of your life and take control of the steering wheel. Don't be afraid; nothing under his control can ever be out of control. Mastered by Christ, you can handle anything."* Unfortunately, during that time of my life, I meticulously selected what to give God, if anything at all. I didn't have time for that. My shift in life had taken place, and *I* was going to determine where the chips would fall, *NOT GOD!*

I walked into my classroom and felt a sense of excitement coupled with nervousness. I was about to teach English to middle school students. I had witnessed my good friend years before fall in love with teaching. Everything was about her students. At times she spent Saturdays and late afternoons pouring into these children. I thought she was crazy and told her as much. "I would not be giving up my Saturdays to these kids, that's what they have parents for." We would laugh, but past the smiles, I saw her passion for education. It was inspiring to me. So, when she told me her school was looking for an English teacher, I jumped at the opportunity to interview and figured I would learn how to teach along the way. My goal was simple, try it out, make more money and spend the summer looking for a new job if I didn't like it. That was over 20 years ago. As time went by, I would find myself mimicking the actions of my friend. There were late days, Saturday field trips, and even school-sanctioned overnight and weekend excursions. These students had become part of the fabric of my life. They filled a void in me. Many of them also mirrored the pain I was determined to tuck away by volunteering for various activities, sponsoring clubs, and using my free time to expose them to things outside of their zip code. They had become my family. As with any family, there were tears and cracks bleeding through the crooked, beautiful smiles that walked across the threshold of my classroom doors each day, and as time went on, I began to learn their stories.

"Good Morning, Welcome to English."

"Good morning." echoed the students as they trailed into my class, taking their seats. "My name is Ms. Campbell, and I will be your 7th Grade English teacher." I pointed to the board so they could see the spelling of my name and class.

"Today, we will learn a little more about each other. I will be taking attendance, reviewing our rules, and then we will complete the *Do Now* posted on the board." I began to arrange the students in alphabetical order and, at times struggled over names but quickly apologized for my mistakes. They appeared to give me grace. After everyone was settled, I walked to the beginning of each row and carefully counted out composition notebooks.

"Please take a notebook and pass the rest back to the person behind you." I looked up to see a student raising her hand.

"Are we keeping these notebooks?"

"Yes. Please write your first and last name on the notebook and your class number that's posted on the board."

"I already have a notebook!" I heard someone yell out.

"These notebooks will not be used for English notes. They will be used as writing journals."

"What's that?"

"Every day, when you come to class, I will have a *Do Now* posted on the board that you will copy into your notebook and write about. At the end of this time, I will collect all notebooks, and they will remain in class, so you have them every day."

"Is this like a diary?" I heard a girl question.

"Yes. I guess you can compare it to a diary."

"Does that mean you expect us to put personal stuff in it?"

"No, I expect you to complete the *Do Now* I post every day that may ask things about you, English or life. Let's look at today's assignment. Please write about your favorite part of this summer. Pick one thing to write about." It was like a light switch turned on and I saw my students eagerly writing in their notebooks. This one simple gesture set the tone for a school year full of reflection and transparency by students. I read their journals and posted comments and questions. Much to my surprise, the students began responding to my comments.

The journal had turned into a conversation. Their transparency of imperfect thoughts, questions, concerns, and admissions served as a mirror and window to those dark places in my soul I refuse to confront and heal. But, as I waded through their written thoughts it felt as if they could see me. Was I showing signs of cracking and collapse? There were stories of dysfunctional relationships, abuse, neglect, addiction, and loss. Some students poured out their hearts and would walk by my desk on their way out of class and whisper, "Please read my journal and write back to me." I received notes on my desk asking, "Are you going to read my journal?" My intrigue opened up a disconnected space in my heart and I began to feel emotions with an urge that would no longer be subdued. Sometimes I would cry during planning periods muffling my sounds of agony, yearning for the one thing I could no longer have–a mother. The strain that I experienced over a lifetime with my father would not be able to fill the empty spaces in my heart. Life for me was lonely even though I was not companionless.

My unwillingness to grapple with the loss began to seamlessly fracture and dismantle friendships and relationships. I did not want to see the shadows. I did not want to experience the brokenness. I did not want to be caught in the sphere of this pain any longer. I did not want to live. Yet each day, I hypocritically leaned into the lives of children who dared to be brave and speak their truth, but I could not.

The final blow would come from the betrayal of a man I loved and trusted. His disloyalty would become like another death to me, a meaningful detachment of someone I loved. Death is death, and the harmfulness of it can't be diluted, diminished or camouflaged in a corner somewhere. My life had exploded, and I began to search for the pieces that would once again make me wholly love myself. Instead of digging within, I sadly reached outside and almost ended up losing myself. I needed to begin living my life from the inside out to survive. I needed to deal with emotions before an ill-timed explosion took place!

"Hello. My name is Carol Campbell and I'm trying to reach Dr. Wagoner to set up an appointment for therapy. Please call me back at... ." It was time to deal with the emotional turmoil that filled spaces so tightly hidden. There was a buzz from the intercom that allowed me to push the door open. I entered, unsure of where to go. I immediately noticed a hallway lined with chairs. I took a seat and counted the four closed doors in front of me. A small table hosting magazines sat next to the chairs. My nerves were jumping all over the place as I grabbed a magazine to calm down. In my mind, I imagined sitting in a room with a long couch or chaise lounge. Would I have to lay down? Would there be lots of questions? Would she be taping our sessions?

After a few minutes, a door opened up and an almost frail woman with a gentle voice and firm handshake greeted me.

"Hello. Please come in."

"Hello."

I walked in, feeling the dry and motionless air that was surrounded by sparsely scattered furniture in a dimly lit room. I sat on the tan couch and could feel the firmness of its pillows along my back. The anxiety of this moment rose in my throat, making my mouth parched. Would I really be able to tell a complete stranger my secrets, my fears, and my deepest, most sacred thoughts? My heart yearned for this moment, but my mind moved with caution. She reviewed the logistics and protocols of the practice before jumping into the safe space of my thoughts.

"What brings you here today?'

"I lost my mother and think it's time to talk about it."

"What has brought you to this moment?" Just like that, a stream of tears came running down my face. I looked over to my left to see a box of tissue waiting to comfort me. I recounted the death of my mother and the end of a long-term relationship. She listened, took notes and directed me down a path I had avoided traveling for over a year. I was feeling lost during the journey and just wanted to find my way home. I no longer wanted to be a reincarnation of myself, it was a shell, it was a lie. I was just existing. Week after week, I sat on that couch, searching for a way to be me again. But the more therapy I had, the more I realized that this journey was not about becoming the "old me." It was deeper. It was taking a dive into feelings that had been lost because they were too painful to endure. This therapy was no longer just about the death of a parent or relationship. It was about the stages of grief and death I had experienced due to molestation and the abandonment I felt from my dad. Those raw emotions of insecurity met me face to face. It was messy work. At twenty-five, I had just begun the stages of self-discovery. I was processing and realizing my worth, discovering my wonderland.

The work to heal was hard and seemed never-ending. I kept trying to get to a destination that seemed unattainable and, at times, frustrating. I continued to do the work, but found myself longing to fill a void of intimate and personal connection. I didn't understand that the job of healing could not afford any distractions. It must be intentional, purposeful, and developmental. It is meant to make you better, but more importantly, it should become the mirror of self-awareness. I can look back now and see how those moments of distraction disillusioned my journey and kept me on a detour from embracing my true self. Twenty-five years later and the irony has not escaped me. This was my pilgrimage through the wilderness.

The excursion was a repetitive occurrence of familiar findings and faults. I just kept taking the same trip without packing my self-awareness. I was still going to therapy but, still compartmentalizing and not realizing that the birth of my new relationship had the residuals of my old one. I would often say to my girlfriends that it felt so comfortable being with this person like I had known him before. The truth is, I did know him before. However, he would bring some additional baggage.

That summer would become significant in so many ways. It was hurried, exciting, and full of new experiences. I met the man who would eventually take me on a rollercoaster ride that I stayed on for three years before getting off. Truthfully the lingering effects took a lot longer than that to be erased. I had hit the trifecta with him—women, gambling and financial instability. It was a whirlwind of lies and more lies. I had completely lost myself in an extremely dysfunctional relationship. It didn't start out that way. We seemed so compatible and in sync. There was laughter and fun. Until there was none. Laughter and fun are great attributes, but those aren't the things that make a good relationship or parents.

It would take the birth of my eldest daughter for me to begin the process of healing again. Only this time, I didn't run to a therapist. I ran to God. I remember being invited by a friend to Thursday night worship at Christian Life Center in Brooklyn. I lived in the Bronx but knew that invitation was not by chance. I felt both compelled and excited to go. It had been a long time since I attended church. I looked around and saw so many people. I was struck by the number of young Black men in attendance and the young beautiful Black women walking around. I had never seen so many Black people in one place unless it was a club or a concert. This was amazing! I sat down with my friend as the service began and became lost in every word, song, and prayer.

In that space, there was a void being filled. I remember softly caressing my stomach and whispering to my baby, "I've found my home." This was my tribe. I promised we would both grow in God together. I wouldn't just send her off to church each weekend like my parents did. I would be there with her! That Sunday, I returned to CLC, and it was even grander than Thursday night worship. As I approached the church, I noticed people lined up around the building. I was confused and wondered what was going on. I stood silently on the line, still trying to figure out the hold-up. The line began to move and stop in slow increments. Eventually, I glanced behind me to see the line had gotten even longer. It was then that I realized that these people were just trying to get into church. I had never seen anything like this. I worshiped that day to give God all the glory, beckoning him to be in my life just as he had been when I was a little girl. My praises didn't fall on deaf ears. A tap on my shoulder from a stranger and an altar invite was all I needed. That Sunday, I gave my life to Christ. When I got home that day, I really looked at myself in the mirror for the first time in years and said *I LOVE YOU!*

Something changed in me. Every Sunday and even some Thursdays, I would make the challenging trip to Brooklyn across the bridge to hear a word. I was reading and studying my bible more. My daughter's dad began to sense a shift in me. Eventually, he began to join me, and I thought we were ascending to a new place that might have saved our relationship. Instead, it exposed the gaping holes. I didn't know how to get out! I was about to become a mother and needed a way out. I needed to love myself more than him. I didn't want the drama anymore and decided to leave. I was sure this was God-ordained. All the ducks lined up for me as I planned for my *new* location: a *new* job, a *new* place, and a *new* church with the help of the CLC family. A few months later,

I packed up my life and moved from the only home I knew. It was bittersweet, but necessary.

My daughter's dad and I were in agreement that he would stay in New York. On the day of moving, that all changed with an announcement to his family and me that he would be moving with me. I was dumbfounded and didn't know what to say. A smile of discomfort eased out. I just stood there and let it all unfold, saying nothing really paralyzed in fear. Then we jumped into the car and a packed U-Haul truck, with all *our* belongings, and drove to Maryland. This was not supposed to be a part of my "I LOVE ME TOUR."

LUNCH
Nourishment for The Body

"You can never find yourself until you face the truth."
–PEARL BAILEY

1. What attitudes or behaviors from childhood have you brought into adulthood? List them.

____

____

____

____

____

____

____

____

____

____

____

2. How has this attitude or behavior impacted your life?

____

____

____

____

____

____

____

____

3. Think about a happy or positive childhood experience and write about it.

____

____

____

____

____

____

____

4. How has that thought, or experience impacted your life today *(If you're an educator, how does it show with your students)*?

5. Today dismantle limiting beliefs of the past and press forward to the change you are creating every day. Embrace your transformation and transition into the beautiful butterfly you were meant to become. Express your creativity by coloring your renewal and evolution below.

6. The road to healing requires support. Take this time to write down one or two favorite quotes, affirmations or scriptures that will anchor you in this journey.

FOURTH PERIOD

ESSENTIAL QUESTION: ***How do we determine our worth?***

We first became acquainted when she attended dance tryouts. She was a spunky girl quick to get an attitude and challenge an adult or child. I liked her. She was not afraid to speak her mind. Sometimes she spoke it just a little bit too much, earning her calls home and various reprimands. When they couldn't get through to her, I would sometimes receive a knock on my classroom door from a teacher telling me about her behavior because she was on my dance team. I quickly learned that year that the best way to make sure my team behaved was to threaten them with not performing at school activities. For the most part, it worked.

Niecey was one of several siblings. I never taught her, but she was always swinging by the classroom, requesting that she be transferred to my class. I thought she was funny. However, beyond that hard exterior was just a kid wanting to be noticed and accepted. On other days she would stop by the class and give me the 411 on the latest drama in our middle school world.

"If she says something to me, I'm punching her in the face, Ms. Campbell!"

"What will that do besides getting you suspended?"

"She better stop playing with me! She's always running her mouth! I swear..."

I would let her continue to vent, hoping that it would calm her down. Then I would gently remind her, "If you get in a fight, you won't be able to perform."

"I hear you, Miss Campbell, but she betta stay outta my way!"

"It's just not worth it."

I wish that there was someone to talk me down off that ledge many times as a kid. I was so quick to fight. Little did Niecey know I understood her more than she realized. I sent her to class and made her promise not to fight. I wasn't sure that would work, but anything was possible.

The great thing about after-school practice is that it kept my team off the street and out of trouble. It was two extra hours I got to keep them safe and out of harm's way. These girls were good dancers and didn't need too much prompting to show up and practice. They were hungry for something to do. They got so excited every time there was an upcoming performance. That next year I would transfer to another school and Niecey would continue to remain a fixture in my life. Her mother would pass away and she would become much more attached. She would come by my new school to visit often, and before I knew it, the staff thought Niecey was my niece. Her visits gave her a space to do homework and avoid hanging out in the streets, even if for a short moment. I didn't mind being that place for her. Now living with her dad, it seemed as if Niecey traveled adrift in unfamiliar surroundings. Before she could really settle into a conscious rhythm of her new environment, Niecey's dad passed away. Once again, familiar with the constant companion of discord, she went to live with an older sister. There were so many shifts that it was only natural that she began to operate in her shadow of strength and protection.

At the same time, I decided to shift my own life and leave New York City. However, when I hit the road to Maryland, Niecey was with me. I was really considering having her live with me permanently. She spent a few weeks with me and things were going well. I was concerned about her going back home. There were times I could overhear conversations that seemed to be dripping with information about illegal activities. I was still trying to figure things out and knew that this was not something I could take on. I needed to get more settled and she needed to stop whatever she was doing. We agreed that she would go live with her sister until I could bring her back. That day never came. My life became more complicated, and she settled into a new life with her older sister.

Years later, I would find out about the abuse she endured at the hands of her sister. My heart was broken to learn how she had been failed by another adult. It would explain the recklessness with which she lived her life. It was clear that her drinking and fighting provided a way to medicate the pain inflicted by another loved one. She was like me, a motherless daughter, *trying to find her worth in this world.*

✳ ✳ ✳ ✳ ✳

I got to Maryland and loved it. However, my relationship was two and a half months of hell. There was arguing, lying, gambling and cheating. There was a *new* baby on the way, and I was *NOT* the mother! When we had come to the end of the road, determined to go our own separate ways, he landed a final blow that had me struggling to survive. I am sure that this journey was orchestrated by God, but like Abraham, I was never instructed to bring anyone with me but my daughter on this excursion. As a result, God had to let me falter to figure it all out again and understand that to love anyone else, I needed to start with myself.

It had been a few days since he left and I was now tasked with securing full-time childcare. I immediately reached out to Ms. Evelyn, who I had been using a couple of days a week so my daughter's father could go on "job interviews." She agreed to watch her all week which also increased the amount I paid for childcare. I sat on the floor of my living room looking at my paystub and wondered how I was going to make ends meet. Although the cost of living was cheaper in Maryland, I had not calculated how much money would come out of my check for healthcare benefits. As a result, for the first time in my life, I had become part of the American statistic, a single parent living paycheck to paycheck.

Thursday afternoon, on my way to pick up the baby, I stopped at the bank ATM to get Ms. Evelyn's money. She was very clear that all her payments were due on Thursday. As I completed the process and waited for the funds, I was startled and shocked by what happened next. The screen read INSUFFICIENT FUNDS. Immediately, I panicked and began doing the process over and over again until I noticed there was a line behind me. I couldn't figure out what had occurred. I ran into the bank, holding back tears and praying for some kind of technical error. I went to see someone in the customer service area and explained my confusion. My heart was beating so hard and my thoughts were scrambling for clarity. After a few minutes, I heard the representative say, "It appears there was a withdrawal from the account on Friday and another one on Saturday morning. Without any warning, the tears flowed down my face.

"Oh my God, he stole from me, I whispered in disbelief."

"Did someone steal from you?" She questioned. At the same time, I could see her offering me tissue paper. "If this is a case of theft, you can report it."

I remember her giving me a few telephone numbers before looking up at the clock, wiping my tears, and rushing to pick up the baby. I was angry. I was scared. I was lost. What was I going to tell Ms. Evelyn?

My nerves rattled and it felt as if my voice was being swallowed in the fear that covered me. I knocked on the door and forced a smile. "Hello."

"Hello." I couldn't really pay attention to her greeting and what she was saying as I tried to construct the right sentences to say in my head.

"Ms. Evelyn, I have a problem. I went to withdraw your money from the bank just now and didn't realize her dad stole all my money. I don't have enough to pay you." As I forced that last bit of information, the tears flowed once again. I was so embarrassed and continued the search in my mind for ways to get money. I could see the hurt in Ms. Evelyn's eyes. I went on to explain that I couldn't pay her until the next Friday. I offered to keep the baby home for the next few days but would still pay her the same amount of money. She agreed. Thursday evening, I called in sick and was out until the following Tuesday.

I got home that night and called my ex-boyfriend's parent's home. He wasn't home, and by the third call, I spilled every detail to his parents.

"Please have him call me. Tell him if I don't hear from him, I will be filing a police report about the money he stole from me."

"What do you mean?"

"Before leaving here, he used my ATM card and stole money from my account. I didn't even have enough money to pay the childcare provider! Why would he do something like that to us? I cried. I just want my money back! I need my money back!" There was silence for a moment.

"I don't know what is going on with him. I will have him call you the minute he comes in here!" I put down the phone receiver and looked around my empty apartment and began to sob. What had I done? Was moving to Maryland a bad idea? My tears soaked the pillow. Once again, my heart broke into a million pieces, just like it had done when I lost my mother. I just wanted to be able to hear her voice telling me what to do. I wanted to be a kid again, being given directions that kept me safe and out of harm's way. But there was no voice, only the echoes of my mind searching for wisdom.

I was awakened by a phone ringing in the distance. I didn't have the energy to get up until it rang again. I mustered the energy to get up! "Hello."

"Hello. This is Diane. I just spoke to Mummy. How are you doing?" In my mind, I didn't want to have this conversation. I also didn't want to be rude. She had always been nice to me. I think in her own way, she always tried to warn me about her brother. I sat there on the phone, listening and filling the air with responses like *no* and *I don't know*. I hated recounting the story all over again; my head was throbbing as the tears crusted around my eyes. As she spoke, it felt like her words just added to the enduring emotional pain that had suddenly turned physically nauseating. I was going to excuse myself from the well-meaning call when I heard her say, "let me send you some money."

"Thank you, but there is no need to do that. I will figure it out."

"Don't be silly; it's the least I could do after what my brother did!"

"Thank you," I whispered as the tears once again showered down my face. Shortly after, we ended the call. It all felt surreal.

I walked over to my daughter's bassinet and just watched as she peacefully slept, oblivious to the storm that was raging in our lives. My mind echoed with futile ideas of what to do next. I was stuck. Reaching out to people meant admitting my failures and poor decision-making skills. The blanket of humiliation was suffocating me and I could not bear to be uncovered. I wasn't ready to reveal my truth yet again to another person. So there I sat and sat on the floor, weeping for a resolution. A resolution never came and my phone never rang again that night.

The next morning felt like a continuation of the night before. I immediately fell into my regular single-parent routine of changing the baby's diaper, washing her up, and cooking her breakfast. I smiled at how excited she became when it was time for her to eat. Her hungry lips clasped the bottle nipple as she feverishly gulped down the sweetness of the cornmeal porridge. I was in my happy place. She eased the sorrows from the evening, and I was lost in my love for her. It was as if the devil became jealous of my content nature because shortly thereafter, a ringing sound jarred me from my peaceful time. The persistent howling began to unnerve me all over again. I scooted over to the phone with the baby in my arms.

"Hello."

"Hello. Yeah, it's me." Instantly, a tension overcame me, and I struggled to remain calm.

"Listen, it's really simple, Western Union my money or I am reporting the theft to the police."

"Listen, I'm sorry. I will give you back your money."

"I don't need your apology…just send me the money."

"I'll send it back on Monday."

"Monday! I screeched. I need my money today. I WANT MY MONEY TODAY!" The baby shifted in my arm as a gentle reminder to keep calm and avoid disturbing her mealtime.

"I won't have it until Monday. Look, what I did was messed up, and I'm really sorry." I listened but didn't care about apologies. I didn't care about anything he was saying. I just wanted my money. I was tired of listening. I was tired of talking…so I stopped and hung up the phone. The phone immediately rang back, but I didn't answer. It rang several more times, and I still didn't answer.

After the last set of rings, I unplugged the phone to avoid hearing from anyone that day. It was going to be just my little girl and me all day. That day I drowned out my pain and anger with music. I played music all day long. I wondered what my neighbor must be thinking as I blasted everything from Biggie to Beres Hammond and everything in between. It was old skool meets new school. Baby girl looked at me with both laughter and confusion. Yes, your mama is filling her soul and drowning her tears with music. Each day after he left, I began to craft a new life for myself. I was in a new city with a new job, a newborn, new debt and no friends. Back then, as I looked at my daughter and the tears rolled down my face, the words of Bob Marley would leave my lips, defying my present and determined to speak my future.

"So no woman, no cry

No woman, no cry

I say, oh little oh little darling, don't shed no tears

No woman, no cry…

Everything's gonna be alright

Everything's gonna be alright

Everything's gonna be alright

Everything's gonna be alright"

NO MORE TEARS TODAY! In a strange way, it was a great day. I began to bask in my freedom. I was free from a toxic relationship and the responsibilities associated with adults.

We would be alright. As I looked at the CD compilation in my hand, it was probably the second-best thing I ever received from him. That song would connect me to the past I journeyed from and the future I was trying to create. Each time I listened, there was another song to direct and lift my spirits, and soon I began to embrace Bob's message: *"Don't worry about a thing, every little thing gonna be alright."* It didn't mean that tough times weren't going to happen, but I would soldier through it.

Monday came and went with no call. Tuesday came with no call and no money. Wednesday came and went too. I stopped waiting for the call and money. Instead, I pushed my pride to the side and reached out to my cousin and borrowed money with a promise to pay it back on a specific day. The next day I opened my mail to receive two checks, one from his sister and the other from a phone company if I switched my service. I endorsed both checks and deposited them. By the end of that week, I had a very important decision to make.

"Hello."

"Hi, Mama." I cried hesitantly to my grandmother.

"How are you and the baby doing?"

"We're okay. Well, not really. I need your help." I broke down and told my grandmother what had happened. She silently listened to me, and at times, I would hear her utter, "Oh, God."

"Momma, can she come and stay with you for a little while?" I just need to find a second job and save some money to get back on my feet.

"Yes, bring her. Come!" she uttered in a voice filled with concern. Two weeks later, we jumped on the highway to New York. Each mile we drew closer to the city I used to call home brought an overwhelming feeling of heartache and nausea. What was I going to do without her for the next six weeks? Once again, I was crying. I waited until the last minute to contact her dad. He had the nerve to be upset and asked me to bring the rest of his things with me. I played it cool and said yes because I knew in order for this to work, he would need to pick up his daughter on the weekends so my grandmother would get a break.

Being at my grandmother's house that weekend seemed surreal. What was she thinking? She was so kind to me and treated me with love. There were no lectures, just love! She looked at her great-granddaughter and smiled and wondered aloud what her daughter, my mother, would say if she was alive.

"Enid would love up this child if she was alive," she chuckled in her hearty Jamaican accent.

"I know. I miss her so much! I cried."

"You just have to do the best you can. God is watching over you!"

As the tears once again streamed down my face. I knew she was right. That night as I closed my eyes and went to sleep in the shadows of my dream, I saw the emotional journey of a woman that looked like me continue to struggle and stay stuck in the shadow of her pain and regret.

FIFTH PERIOD

ESSENTIAL QUESTION: *When does a house become a home?*

This was the hub. This was the center where multiple ideas and people connected to share lives in a single network–education. This was the pulse where minds were molded for adults and children alike. Even on a good day, our education never stayed in the four walls of any one classroom. It usually spilled into hallways, offices, and outside in neighborhoods. The neighborhood was also a classroom. It held the rise and fall of many of our students as they journeyed along nondescript streets, corner stores and collective alleys and walkways. Each day children, as well as adults, strolled into our buildings, touting their smiles, attitudes, disappointments, or anger. It was my job as an administrator to navigate a friendly approach despite my own feelings. One day as I circled the hallways doing the usual morning pleasantries, I noticed a student approaching me, looking a little disheveled in her uniform. As she got closer, I immediately turned her around in our unspoken language and escorted her to my office. We sat down with the silence and the sounds of tears being sniffled between each breath. I handed her some tissue and turned down my walkie-talkie to quiet the ongoing banter of conversations swirling around the school.

"Patrice, what's going on?"

"My aunt put me out."

A baffled "Why?" escaped my mouth.

"She doesn't want me there anymore. I am going to live with my grandfather."

"Where does he live?"

"DC."

"Give me your grandfather's number." This move to DC meant we had to transfer her out of the school. At that moment, I knew that her world had already changed enough and to put her out of school would be devastating. I needed to immediately put some things in place so that wouldn't happen.

Patrice came to us in 7th grade as a tough girl with a "chip on her shoulder" that seemed hard to knock off. Her mouth could be reckless and her attitude was never too far behind. I saw past the gruff exterior and knew she was much more than those words she spat out to reduce other kids to a small size. I remember when she showed up for my step team tryouts with her friends. I wasn't surprised. However, I knew, within the first 30 minutes, only she and one other girl would make the cut. She was swift, smart and talented. I looked forward to her bringing that energy to step because I believed it could be molded into something positive. I was right. She caught on to routines quick and her movements exuded confidence as she practiced and helped others teammates learn the various steps. More importantly, her grades were good as she often made the Honor Roll. I was so proud of her progress. Being able to practice and perform in various competitions helped to shift some of that attitude. It wasn't fully gone. But, she knew discipline referrals would have her doing extra in practice or benched. We were more than half-way through her 8th-grade year and I knew transferring her to another school would be detrimental to the progress we had made. I wasn't about to let that happen!

As I looked into her face, it was obvious that sending her to class was not a good idea. Instead, I sent her to Ms. Lawrence's office and had the classwork sent over. In the meantime, I headed to see the guidance secretary. "Ms. Davis, what steps do I need to take if a student has become homeless?"

"Their parents have to fill out the paperwork."

"The parent is not in the picture. The student was living with a relative who put her out."

"Where is she now?"

"She went to stay with her grandfather." I knew what she was going to say next as her eyes peered over the glass that laid tightly on her face.

"She would have to go to the school in her grandfather's neighborhood." I knew that wasn't an option. I thanked her and moved on to my next stop. Keeping Patrice at the school would require permission from my principal.

Mr. Miller and I had a pretty good relationship. More importantly, he had a sincere love for the students we served. I had seen him be stern and empathetic in one breath when disciplining a child. In my heart, I knew he would help me keep her at our school. I eased myself into his office to share what was happening. The one thing I knew my principal appreciated was sharing a solution for every problem. So as I explained the problem, I was sure to offer a solution. As I hoped, he gave me the go-ahead to put my plan in motion. I hurried myself to the guidance conference room and called Patrice's grandfather. I let him know that she would be coded as a homeless student because she was put out of her aunt's house. However, as a homeless student, she would still be able to attend the school. We just needed him to come and fill out the necessary paperwork. Patrice had finally found her home.

$$* \quad * \quad * \quad * \quad *$$

The days and weeks seemed so long as I did my best to survive and occupy myself without my daughter. I probably cried myself to sleep every night for six weeks. I felt like such a failure. To make things worse, her dad had not been consistent in picking up the baby every weekend, like he promised. So my grandmother ended up caring for her more than she planned. She would tell me it was okay because, at least this way, she knew her granddaughter was safe.

In Maryland, I had to change a lot about the way I lived. Money was so tight that I eventually had to opt out of medical coverage from my job. Each day I lived in fear. What if the baby got sick? What if I got sick? I was a single mother and everything was on me. It was a path I had walked before, but back then, I was the child of a single parent. Everything about my life at that moment reminded me of the empty promises my mother often shrugged off from my father. With the lack of support from her dad, I continuously walked around in a bubble of fear and anxiety. Every week I searched for part-time jobs. I signed up for extra-curricular and after-school activities. They offered the extra money I needed. Unfortunately, those payments didn't come until the middle and end of the year.

One day, I overheard one of the secretaries talking about her part-time job at a local university. I'm not sure what made me do it, but I asked if she knew of any other positions. When she said yes, my eyes lit up. The next week I was interviewing, and the following week I was hired as a front desk receptionist at George Washington University. It was an easy job that I did in the evenings and every other Saturday. It helped me financially but still wasn't enough. It did allow me to save a little money before going to pick up my daughter in New York.

Ever since her dad stole my money, I played a constant game of catch-up each month. The bills were late and always had additional fees added to them. I would come home to find threatening notices on my door about the rent. I would call the rental office and listen to their warnings about paying my rent as soon as possible. I had never been in such a situation, and beneath all the smiles lived a very frightened person who wanted to just scream. I felt so alone. There were days I would enter my apartment on a Friday after work and cry, sitting in the corner of an empty living room all weekend as I gazed upon the blue, white and colorful makeshift curtains I created out of sheets and a blanket to cover the patio door windows. I left a completely furnished condo in the Bronx to end up like this. I'm sure my mother was in the heavens *shaking her damn head* and wondering what happened to her daughter. This was some next-level shit. I had nothing but two bedroom sets I brought with me from New York. Truth be told, Mommy bought those too!

One morning I woke up for the first time in months and the crying began to slow down. I felt an energy that hadn't been present in a long time. Maybe it was having my daughter back home with me or the friendships I had created in such a short amount of time. I was beginning to see hope and feel encouraged. I finally found a church in the area to attend and my colleague Alease would often pray for and with me. She was married with one child and another on the way. I had so much respect and admiration for her walk with God. It was authentic and not judgmental to people like me who didn't always fall in line with the rules of Christianity. One day she shared a devotional with me, *Time With God*, that literally made those very hard days more bearable. I would read it and feel a sense of peace come over me. It was in those moments that the promise I made to my baby about returning to life with Christ at the helm seemed possible. We were making it. I found a clinic to take her to that provided a sliding scale for visits. To this day, I believe the woman who put in my information did it wrong because my co-pay was so low.

One day in the midst of my animated instruction, a staff member came to tell me there was an emergency phone call for me in the office. Back then, teachers did not have phones in their classrooms, just an intercom. Immediately my mind went to the baby, *Oh God, What could be wrong?* I rushed to the phone so quickly, panting and out of breath. "Hello!"

"Hello, is this Ms. Campbell?" In my mind, I thought, this doesn't sound like the babysitter.

"Yes, who is this?"

"This is Fran from Universal Apartments." Oh No, I thought to myself, someone has broken into the apartment.

"Yes, is something wrong with the apartment?"

"I'm actually calling to let you know that the Marshals will be going out to your apartment today to put your things out. I just wanted to inform you so that your things aren't sitting out on the street. Are you able to get to the property and get your things?" Her words were swirling around my head. What the hell was she saying?

I was stunned, stuck and stammered out, "I am at work and need to find a way home. Can you please call me back when the Marshals get there?"

I stood in the copy room of the main office fighting back tears. The secretaries were at their desks, and I didn't want to break down in front of them. I hung up the phone and eased into the staff bathroom next door. I turned on the water and began to cry my eyes out. "What am I going to do?" is all I kept mumbling over and over again. I heard the doorknob and immediately thought my crying was louder than I thought. However, it was just someone checking to use the bathroom. I slowly grabbed the paper towel, wet it and wiped my face. I stared in the mirror, searching my face for the strength I needed to get through this moment. My hands trembled and my body shook from the fight that took a hold of me. As I calmed myself to be still, I dried my face and headed to the principal's office. I had a class full of students waiting for me to come back and teach them. I knocked on her door and was directed to come inside.

I sat down, squeezing the wad of tissue balled up in my hand. "Ms. Lane, I can't go back to class and teach today." Before she could even ask me, what was going on, I broke down and cried again.

"I just received a call from the property manager at my apartment complex and they are putting me out today. I have to find a place for me and my daughter." I held my head down in my embarrassment.

"Where is your fiancé?" she whispered.

"We broke up months ago and stole my money which is why I have fallen behind on my bills."

"Okay. Is there anyone you can call?"

"I do have one person that I can call. I'm so sorry to have to leave my class."

"Ms. Campbell, that is not a problem. You do what you have to do. Is it okay if I bring Ms. Christian in here and tell her what's going on? She may know of some organizations and churches that might be willing to help you." I felt myself swallow down an objection. At this point, my pride was already scraping the bottom of the barrel. Ms. Christian was the school's Guidance Counselor and a colleague. She was always warm and kind. Deep down, I knew she could be helpful to me. Plus, I had limited options. Ms. Lane left me in her office and went to speak with Ms. Christian. A few minutes later, they both reappeared, and I could see the empathy in their eyes. I knew they weren't judging me.

They just wanted to help! Ms. Christian and I walked over to her office. "Do you have anyone you want to call?"

"Yes. There is one person."

"Okay, I am going to lunch duty and you stay in here and make all the calls you need to."

"Thank you." I immediately picked up her phone and called the one person I knew well in the area. I called Eliza, favorably known as Aunt Lizzie. She was the cousin of my ex-boyfriend from years before. However, we always remained friendly and in touch. She was still my Aunt Lizzie. When I could not reach her at home. I decided to call her at work. She had been a longtime employee of Verizon and I just knew it was going to be easy to find her. After bouncing around from several different offices looking for Aunt Lizzie and mispronouncing her last name somehow, I was able to connect with her. She was more than happy to open her home to me. It was like the light at the end of a tunnel. Unfortunately, I forgot that Aunt Lizzie didn't drive and she was located way down in Virginia. I was stuck again. Although I drove and had a car, what no one knew was that my car had been repossessed a week earlier. Instead, I told people my car was in the shop being fixed and a colleague agreed to give me a ride to work. I sat there in the office looking at the phone and wondering what the next step would be for us. Ms. Christian entered her office and asked if things had worked out. I shook my head *no* and sat there looking at the time. I had to think of something before the day ended.

"Why don't we call the church?" About a month before, I had started attending the same church, New Horizon. A knot formed in the pit of my stomach as I digested the thought of having to share my story with yet another person, but pride had moved away hours ago. I listened as she spoke to someone on the other end and then handed me the phone. I took a deep breath and explained the story again. There was an uneasy silence on the other side of the phone.

The voice finally said, "How long have you been attending our church?"

"One month," I said, confused.

"You know it's very important to balance, budget, and save your money so that these types of things won't arise! As a single mother, this is a very important lesson for you to remember."

"I understand that, and unfortunately, I have not been able to do that due to unforeseen circumstances with her dad."

"Yes, I understand. Unfortunately, because you are new and recently became a member, we are unable to help you at this time. If you would like to reach out in a few months, we may be able to better assist you." I was stunned at the cold and callous way she shared the information. I didn't think anyone could break me down anymore that day. But in an instant, I was reduced to rubble and felt like shit! As I looked across the desk to Ms. Christian, I could see and feel the disappointment and irritation in her face. My next call was to local shelters that would take in mothers and babies. Other than making calls to people when my mother died, this was by far the second hardest thing I've ever done. I followed that up with an equally difficult call to the property manager who told me the Marshals were still on their way. I HAD FAILED AT MY JOB AS A MOTHER, AND IT BROUGHT ME TO THIS MOMENT AND TIME. I WAS ABOUT TO LOSE EVERYTHING!

As the school day ended, my principal called me to her office to see my progress.

"Were you able to come up with any resolutions?"

"Yes, I was able to find a shelter that would take my daughter and me." Her eyebrows furrowed and forehead wrinkled in sadness. I could see the pain and disbelief in her eyes.

"I want to thank you for everything you did today. I probably won't be at work tomorrow or the next day until I figure out what to do and where to go next. I am so sorry for any inconvenience," I wept.

"Ms. Campbell, the last thing I'm going to do is let you leave here without a plan. Now, before you say anything, please hear me out. Today, I shared with the staff that one of their colleagues needed our help. I asked them to make a donation. Listen, I did not share the name, but this is what we collected and I am hoping this will help you! I know you're down here with no family, but we are your family, she exclaimed." She placed the envelope in my shaking hands and whispered, "Go take care of that baby and call me later to let me know your status." I left the office eager to get to my child and apartment. I had also reserved a U-haul just in case I needed it. I sat in my colleague's office, waiting for a ride home. In the process of gathering her things, she said, "Hey, did you donate to the person who needed money?"

I formed my words to answer the question, but instead began to cry yet again and mumbled, "That was me!" Once again, I was telling my story. Instead of pity, she gave me something so much more, a shoulder to cry on followed by a loan of $275. 00 in coins that needed to be repaid before the end of the school year. I will never forget how she rushed me to pick up my daughter and up the highway to get my things off the street. I remember turning onto the back road of Lakecrest Drive, holding my breath and looking for my belongings on the street. We neared my building and there was nothing sitting on the curb. I directed her to drive towards the front of the complex expecting to see my things in the parking lot. Again, there was nothing outside. We immediately drove to the rental office, and I ran inside.

"Hello, may I speak to Fran?" A thin, small framed woman, walked out of her office.

"Hello, how may I help you?"

"My name is Carol Campbell and you called me earlier about the Marshals putting my things out."

"Yes, they got held up at another property and will be here tomorrow."

"Can I still pay my rent?" I said in an urgent voice.

"Yes. You can still pay your rent." I went into my pocket and began counting out the cash.

"We can't accept cash. You have to bring us a money order or a cashier's check."

"Okay. I will run to the bank and be back!"

I got in Lisa's car and told her the good news. We made our way to the bank to get a cashier's check and deposit the loose coins we had rolled up. After paying my rent, I still had enough money to get my car back.

That night I entered my apartment with a new found love. I had a home. I had never imagined being homeless. Today I was 30 minutes away from it. I was minutes away from losing all my material possessions. I knew that day would be the last time I ever underestimated the power of God! I would hit other bumps along this journey called life, but deep in my heart I knew that the power of GOD would always prevail!

SIXTH PERIOD

ESSENTIAL QUESTION: *How do educators and students create life-long alliances?*

Beginning in 6th grade, Patrice always felt the burden of inconsistency. She had moved from home to home and felt the pain of instability. On a deeper level, she felt unwanted. She tried to reconcile the thoughts of abandonment in her mind. She lived in a perpetual state of anxiety that only impaired her trust. By the time she moved in with an aunt and was sent to our school, chronic stress and fear had become her familiar place. As a result, by the time she attended our school, all those fears laid at the root of her insecurity which was often covered up by aggressive communication. Years later, I would learn of the abuse she suffered at the hands of her aunt. It made me realize that being kicked out of her aunt's home saved her life.

As Patrice closed out the last year of middle school, we became her adopted village. It was our version of wraparound services. I refused to let her get grabbed up by the statistics that were out in the streets waiting with open arms. She had become an unwritten responsibility that I welcomed. Each week she showed up to school invested in doing well.

She was determined to keep her Honor Roll status. Each quarter as I checked report cards for my step team members, she was always recognized for good grades. She was so proud of that accomplishment. I secretly cheered each quarter that she didn't become a statistic. I understood, intimately, how hard it was to stick to the script of "success" when you're yearning to fill the void of a mother. I knew there were times she was walking a tightrope between success and being sucked into that street life. Her emotions were raw and fragile but covered up with a defensive demeanor that was easily covered in a series of sharp words, eye-rolling, and neck turning. I understood how that hollowness could turn into anger and scattered emotions that stayed stuck–hard to heal.

As fall shifted to spring, the school year began to welcome a time for pomp and circumstance. It was the season to celebrate students graduating from the 8th grade. Our goal was to ensure that all students eligible for promotion would be prepared. In our school, preparation was more than academics and behavior–it was financial. Each year we dug into our own pockets and sought to pour into the lives of well-deserving students in a different but very important way. It was a love gift to ensure no child was ever truly left behind. This year the village chose Patrice. We looked past the hard exterior to see a young girl who was smart and had potential but needed to be seen and feel love, even if it was from strangers. I can remember the day I called her Grandfather to make the arrangements.

The phone rang, and I heard the voice on the other end, "Hello."

"Hello, this is Ms. Campbell from school." I could hear a slight apprehension in his voice as he responded.

I quickly rushed to announce, "She's not in trouble." His hearty laugh warmed my heart. "I wanted to reach out because we would like to purchase Patrice's end-of-the-year necessities for the dance and graduation. However, I wanted to make sure that it was okay with you."

He gleefully responded, "Yes, and thank you!" There was something about his spirit that I just adored. He was a man of a *certain age who stepped in to take care of his great-granddaughter when she had no place to go. His love for her was undeniable and his hope for her future was evident. Although nothing or no one can ever fill the void of missing parents, I continued to hope that her granddaddy's love would saturate the empty spaces. Additionally, I hoped that the love we were showering her way would make her feel less disconnected from a world that often left her out in the cold. I was careful to share our news with Patrice in a way that wouldn't make her feel like a charity case. I will forever remember the smile that cascaded across her face as she beamed with both excitement and appreciation. In the weeks to come, we would purchase clothing, shoes, and ensure her hair and nails were done. There was a sense of pride that echoed throughout "the village" as we made sure that she was treated like one of our own children. The school year would end and Patrice would move on. It was a bittersweet moment. I was excited but nervous for her journey. I wasn't sure how she would navigate the next four years of her life.*

In an effort to keep her closely connected to a support system, one of the people from "the village" agreed to have Patrice live with her. Ms. Johnson was a substitute teacher at our school. She, like me, had grown fond of Patrice and wanted to see her succeed. Moreover, we believed that this arrangement would continue to give her a sense of stability. She continued to live with granddad but stayed with Ms. Johnson for school purposes. The transition had its ups and downs. However, one thing was clear: Ms. Johnson and her family loved Patrice. Ultimately, the strain of differences would become challenging, and she would move back with her granddad full-time and transfer to a school in Washington, DC. Through it all, I made sure to remain a constant in her life. I fussed, scolded, comforted, cheered, and supported her the best way I could. There came a time I knew that she had to be the one to figure it all out.

She was living in Washington DC, trying to navigate a new environment. Eventually, she got tired of fighting others and decided to fight for herself. I will always remember the pride that exuded from her face as she exclaimed, "Ms. Campbell, I am going to graduate early! I am taking classes early in the morning to help me graduate in three years!" She had pivoted. Her energy was enthusiastic as she described goals that included getting straight A's and going to college. She had matured and realized that at this point in her life, she could no longer blame the father she didn't know or the mother who wasn't around. To go down that path would only put her on the same road as the very people she vowed to be different from. Her hard work would pay off as she would graduate high school in three years and be one of the top 10 students with the highest GPA in that graduating class. Before arriving at Avondale Middle School as an administrator, they were people who had whispered warnings of caution to me about the school's problematic environment and students. I often smile, thinking about how one's perception can be out of sync, distorting the success that lies ahead.

The relationship between an educator and a student can sometimes forge unexpected alliances. The work of an educator who is compassionate about the students they serve always starts in the heart. We have a responsibility to help children manage the levels of stress they may be feeling while providing them with academics to excel. The funny thing is many of us need this same support. We are continuously stretched like rubber bands loaded with potential energy that begin to wane after a while and just like that rubber band, we begin to become worn out or, in worst-case scenarios, WE SNAP!

I was worn out, but refused to snap. My life and journey were no longer a solo project. I had a little girl depending on me. She needed my "mommy resilience" to break through the unwelcomed strains and chains that sought to restrain my progress. In the midst of the disruption, I decided to shift, change and own the narrative. It was as Dr. Viktor Frankel states, *"When we are no longer able to control a situation, we are challenged to change ourselves."*

That moment of clarity that is revealed when homelessness is at your doorstep awakened me in a way I never imagined. I began to research next steps to advance my career in education. I was relentless and looked up everything on becoming an administrator. It was time to serve students and families on a different level that would still feed my soul and increase finances. Almost immediately, I began to close the gap on this journey by going back to school and taking on more leadership responsibilities at work. I was the epitome of a purpose-driven life. Nothing was more important to me and things had to change.

The first change in my life would come with where I lived. In a carefully prepared letter, I notified Universal Apartments that I would not be renewing my lease. The hunt for a new place to live was excruciatingly painful. There was the pressure of moving in 60 days and finding a suitable place. It seemed like I fell into one of two buckets, unable to afford or unable to ensure we would live safely in certain places. A good friend of mine had moved into a complex that was both reasonably priced and livable. I was excited to put in my application. Two days later, it was turned down because of my living history at Universal Apartments. Upon receiving the rejection letter, I decided to push forward and reach out to the property manager.

"Hello, how can I help you today?"

"I wanted to meet with the property manager about my rental application."

"What is your name?"

"Carol Campbell," I said in an assertive voice, trying not to let my nervousness show.

"Just a minute. Let me pull your application." I looked as she struck the keyboard and clicked through several computer screens and finally paused, slowly scrolling through one. "Yes, I see your application. Due to your rental history, we are unable to move forward with offering you an apartment for rent."

"Yes, I know that is why I wanted to speak with someone. I was hoping to explain the negative credit history."

"The property manager doesn't usually speak with prospective tenants."

"I know this is an unusual request, but I just wanted to share what happened in my life that caused my failure to pay rent on time." With that, I began to explain my ordeal as a single parent in a new city who was a victim of theft by a loved one. A cloud of embarrassment overcame me, but pride had to be put to the side so my daughter and I could live free from financial struggle. I recounted my story squeezing back tears that seemed to fill every pocket of my eyes until they flooded out without cease. In that moment, I could feel a shift connecting me to the woman across the desk from me. I was no longer just a prospective tenant. I had a name and a face. I became the person behind the application.

"When did you want to move?"

"I was hoping to move in July."

"Your application shows you want into a 2-bedroom apartment. We don't have any of those available. Would you be interested in a 1-bedroom apartment?"

"Yes!" I replied without hesitation.

"I will set up a meeting with the property manager. He has to approve your application. Just share your story with him when you meet. He will be here on Tuesday at 2:00. Can you come at that time?"

"Yes!" I replied again without hesitation. This would mean taking off a half-day from work, but I didn't care. I needed to get this apartment.

A week later, I would meet with the property manager, who would approve my rental application coupled with a letter from me stating that rent would never be late. It was the best thing that could have ever happened. I would live in that apartment for the next four years, always paying rent on time and building my credit along the way. Eventually, the girl who was once at the doorsteps of homelessness would one day be moving from that 1-bedroom apartment to buying her first house. As I continued to work two jobs and complete courses needed to be eligible for a leadership position at work.

That summer, I began taking courses at Trinity University and in the fall, was accepted into the school system's leadership program. It was an extremely busy time as I pursued a position as an Assistant Principal. I also spent much of my time studying for the ISLLC Licensure exam, which was needed to become a school leader. The next 18 months were all about books and budgeting. I had to pay for classes out of pocket and hoped to get a reimbursement from the school system. It was very frustrating as I was always praying that the *pot* of money would not run out before submitting my requests. Reimbursements were given on a first-come, first-serve basis. It was tedious rushing my transcripts to the local school board office, but

I refused to trust the snail mail. Each time I eagerly awaited to receive the news that my reimbursement would occur.

During this time, relationships were not even a thought. Here and there, a date popped-up, but nothing serious. My baby, books, and building a new life were my only focus. Her dad was a thing of the past and only became relevant on my visits back to New York, where he would see her. Financial support was almost non-existent. On one rare occasion, while I was visiting, he asked that we meet so he could buy her some things. Those things turned into a pair of boots and a couple of outfits, but nothing else. As we sat in the store, I worked on being civil to someone who had stolen from me and three years later had yet to return my money.

Looking at him, I asked, "Is there a time when you will begin helping with your daughter?" He gave me a quizzical look and said in hushed tones, "I'm still trying to get on my feet, so I don't have a lot of money yet."

"Okay. Do you think you're able to pay for her dance class? I need her to do some type of extracurricular activity.

"How much is it?"

"It's $35.00 a month."

"I don't think I'll be able to do that," he uttered.

As I heard yet another excuse, I snapped, "That's the difference between us, you do what you can; I do what I can't because there is no opportunity for me to opt out!" He looked at me with intentional sorrowful eyes, but I was not moved. Instead, I just accepted the rare provision of boots and clothing he bought for my daughter. At that moment, my mind began to rev with a silent renewed energy to pursue his active participation in her life one way or another. This would be the last time I would ever beg for his help. That week after returning home, I drove to the child support office and completed the necessary paperwork for him to be involved in her life, if only financially.

I knew this decision would further drive a wedge between him and us. He was not going to be happy with my move to obtain child support regularly. However, for the first time since we had separated, I DID NOT CARE! I did not make this baby by myself. He was a part of every decision made prior to her birth. Naive Carol was no more! I had come to understand the importance of watching a person's actions, not just listening to their words. That day as I sat in the office answering every question and completing every page of the child support request, the words of a good friend kept running through my mind, *"We teach others how to treat us!"* It became a disruptive sound reverberating in my head and with each echo, the notion of having him finally take responsibility was worth the battle. I had spent almost six years in a doldrum, listening to empty promises and hoping for something different each time. I had taught him that his behavior was acceptable. In return, he taught me a critical lesson that the way I treated and valued myself had set the standard for his actions. The realization of this permission gauged, altered, and changed how I would deal with men moving forward.

One day as I was getting the mail, my eye caught the return address of Maryland's Child Support Agency. I rushed into the house to open the letter. A feeling of overwhelm, sorrow and joy consumed me as I read that the child support request had been approved. Little did I know that the approval was one thing, but procuring funds would be *a beast* to secure. The journey to receive child support would take years. For the next several months and years, our lives would endure inconsistent payments. I was unable to rely on or plan that the money from her dad would ever be available. Instead, I began to grapple with the unknown every month. I never knew if a check was coming or if it would be for the amount ordered in the support. Once again, I watched as a system set up to service and maintain the needs of children living with single parents struggled to keep her father committed to his obligations. I continued being the primary caretaker and breadwinner. It came to the point that I stopped hoping and looking for the sky-blue colored check that was supposed to come each month in the mail. Instead, I resigned myself to receiving nothing. This helped ease the pain of disappointment and lowered my expectations.

After several months of receiving no money, I decided to do my research and contacted the Child Support Agency. Each time I reached out to the representatives in my state, no one really had an answer. They took my information, submitted a request to New York, and the cycle of waiting and watching would begin again. My child support request had been considered an interstate case because her dad lived in New York. I often heard people say the bureaucracy of dealing with the child support agency is unbearable. However, I tend to think that it's less about the agency than about the fathers and mothers unwilling to do their jobs as parents. At least, that was my story. Early one Monday morning, I sought to change that narrative.

"Welcome to the New York City Child Support Line. For English, please press 1!"

"If you are a parent or guardian, please press 1."

"Please enter your social security number." I continued to click and follow the commands as directed.

"Please standby as we connect you to the first available agent." I sat on the phone listening to the ominous recorded messages wondering what would happen next? It felt like time stood still. Finally, a live person came on the line and introduced themselves.

"How can I help you today?"

"I live in Maryland and have an established child support case in New York City and want to know the status of it."

"Ma'am, you have to contact your state to receive the current status of your case."

"I have contacted my state, and they didn't have any information."

"I just need to know if her father is still supposed to be paying child support. Has the case been dropped?"

"Yes, there is an active enforcement case."

"Okay. I haven't received child support for several months and would like to know if there is anything I need to do. Why isn't he paying?"

"Ma'am, I am unable to see that information."

"Is there anyone I can talk to about the case?"

"Please hold, and I'll see who can help you." After a short hold, "Ma'am, I'm going to transfer you to someone else who may be able to help you."

"Thank you."

"Hello, this is Sarah Thompson. How may I help you?"

"Hello. I am following up on my child support case. I live in Maryland and haven't received any child support in several months and wanted to know the case status and why my daughter's father isn't paying?"

"Can I have the case number? Can I have your social? Please give me a minute to locate and review the file." Again, I was put on hold. However, in the midst of my anxiety, I realized that each delay brought me closer to answering my questions. So, I waited. I kept thinking to myself, *he has a good job, why won't he pay the child support order?* I was jarred out of my thinking by the voice of Ms. Thompson.

"According to the information submitted, he lost his job and that's why the payments have not been made." My heart sank and tears began to flow without consent. I struggled to speak.

"He has no job?"

"Yes. That's what it states here."

"I'm so tired," I cried. "It's always something, and in the meantime, my daughter suffers."

"I'm so sorry, Ma'am. Please know he is still required to pay, but you may not receive full payments until he starts working again."

"Thank you so much for the information." I walked over to my daughter's bed that morning and watched her sleeping body lying there without a care in the world. I hoped it would always be that way, but I knew that life was never that way.

The moment had me so committed to achieving my goals. After months of full and part-time jobs and taking administrative classes, my time would come. I became fully certified as an Administrator. I didn't have time to rejoice because the road to finding a position would not be easy, but I was determined. For months, the journey included sending resumes, making phone calls, sitting in interviews and seeking mentorship from various educators. When the new school year rolled around, I had not become an Assistant Principal but did begin a new job as a Reading Specialist. My principal knew of my desire to become an AP and promised to refer me out if he ever heard about any positions. That day did come, almost six months after receiving my certification, an interview came my way. I studied all the available data about the school and was prepared. I would be offered the position my birthday, October 26. This moment would forever change the trajectory of the life my daughter and I would live. It was the moment I began to breathe again.

SEVENTH PERIOD

ESSENTIAL QUESTION: *Why do we have to fall apart to become whole?*

She was one of the first people to greet me when I began working at Avondale Middle School. She was small in stature and often donned a hard exterior. However, she was funny to me. I noticed that students seem to really like and respect her. Sometimes her words were quick, smart and laced with reckless sarcasm, but the kids would laugh it off and keep on moving. I also knew that her satirical comments were a way of getting attention from others.

As time went on, I noticed a shift and swings in her behavior. She would go from pleasant to angry and all the emotions in between. Each morning that our paths crossed, I wasn't sure who I would encounter. It was a gamble. Would she be cheerful? Would she be the person who seems to have the world on her shoulder? I continued to pay attention and discussed the changes with my principal.

One day I received an SOS call from my principal. As I rushed into his office, I could see the look of both concern and outrage on his face.

"I need you to sit in here with me as I meet with Ms. Percy. I believe she has come to school under the influence. Please let me know if you smell any alcohol when she comes in here."

"Okay," I uttered in a stunned voice. I had never known of a teacher coming to school under the influence. I took my seat on one

of the chairs in his office. In my mind, I was thinking about keeping my face expressionless. I was jarred out of my thoughts as a small rap came from behind the office door.

"Hello, I was told you wanted to see me." As she sat down, a strong odor of alcohol emitted from her that could be smelled throughout the room.

"Ms. Percy, are you okay this morning?"

"I'm okay. I just didn't sleep good last night."

"Ms. Percy, have you been drinking?"

"No, I went out last night!"

"Well, Ms. Percy, there is a strong odor of alcohol emanating from you."

"It must be my shirt from last night."

"That may be so, but we can't have you smelling like alcohol around the students and I need you to go home."

"But, I am okay," she whined.

"No, you're not. You are not at your best and can't give our kids what they need today. I need you to go home and get yourself well. We will put a sub in your class." With that, she got up from her chair apologetically and left the office to go home. That incident would set off a series of events to come that would show a woman in pain, struggling with addiction, and the inability to take care of her children or eventually keep her job. As a child, I never thought that the adults that taught or monitored me on a daily basis could be suffering and experiencing any anguish. They were just people in the front of a class, monitoring a hallway or taking up space in an office. Their life didn't have any experiences, there was no human

connection for me. Funny how times have changed. Today, I know them. I live them. I connect with every bit of their human souls.

Throwing myself into work and students has always served as my go-to place. Being with students created a barrier, even if only temporarily, to the pain that was determined to creep into my senses. Over the years, I continued to excel as an educator in many roles, from teacher to eventually Principal. Becoming the Principal at a local middle school was a sweet spot for me. At the time, I thought it marked the ultimate accolade to my mom and imagined her approving smile shining down.

It seems like yesterday that I received a phone call about two middle schools who were interested in me as their principal. I had researched both schools thoroughly and knew either one would be a good fit for me. After careful consideration, I chose the school that appeared to be a little rougher around the edges. It had a history of revolving principals, bad publicity, and challenging students. As my husband discussed the possibility, I remember he looked at me in a quizzical manner and said, "Let's take a ride! I need you to see where the school is located before you make a decision." He had grown up in Washington, DC, and was very familiar with the area, and by the looks on his face, I could tell he wasn't sold on the school.

As we drove from Maryland into DC, there was a shift in the vibe and environment. It reminded me of my days of working in the South Bronx. There was that urban feel and city grit that, in some ways, made it feel like home to me. The Bronx was considered one of the poorest boroughs in New York City. However, I didn't see it that way. For me, it was rich with culture and a pulse that kept a steady beat of innovation. The flavor was similar in Southeast DC.

I was not shocked by the projects, homeless people or the pop of culture often sprinkled amid the neighborhoods. There was a rhythm to it that was familiar. The last decade in Maryland had me a little spoiled with pampered students and often permissive parents with their nice cars and even nicer homes. Those students had their share of problems, but it was nothing like I encountered while teaching in the Bronx. For many of my students, their lives were in constant survival mode. I knew from looking around the neighborhood that a little bit of the Bronx lived here.

As we made the left on Stanton Road and drove up the hill, I heard my husband say, "Damn! It has changed around here! There used to be nothing but projects up on this hill!" I looked at the townhouses lining the street that showed no signs of project living except for two buildings on the backside of the school. I looked at the paved sidewalks and lush green grass in certain areas and only one thing popped into my mind—another area of gentrification had taken over the city. For many blacks, that would mean looking for homes elsewhere. We continued driving up and down various streets in the neighborhood, observing the people who were "out and about." Nothing alarming stood out to us. I was pleasantly surprised. That day before we even got back on the highway to head home, I knew this would be my school. The challenge of the school, not its neighborhood, intrigued me!

Over the next few weeks, I began getting myself up to speed on the school. One day while reviewing various pieces of data, an uneasiness came upon me as I recognized the deep work that needed to be done. My heart broke as I saw the disparity in standardized test scores. Had I been removed from these communities for so long that I forgot how deep and wide the "achievement gap" stretched for little black and brown children? I knew that the "socioeconomic gap" of these students also played a part in their struggle to progress. However, in that moment, even amidst my anxiety and fear of failure, I was willing to take the chance.

In July, I made my acquaintance with the school up-close and personal. In his own protective manner, my husband once again drove me to school. This time he waited outside in the car while I walked around the building. Other than the Assistant Principal, no one else knew I was coming into the building. I wanted to see everyone in action doing their daily tasks. It was clear that summer cleaning and some type of renovations were going on as their furnishings were out of place, cleaning items were widely visible, and various fixtures laid around in boxes. I stifled my excitement and nervousness. Everything still felt surreal.

An invisible grin covered my face as I walked into the main office. I stood at a makeshift counter of gray file cabinets and waited for someone to greet me. "Hello, how can I help you?" a voice echoed from behind the desk.

"I am here to see Mr. James."

"Is he expecting you?"

"Yes."

"What's your name?" Hesitantly, I said my name.

"Aren't you the new principal?"

"Yes."

"Welcome." Before I could fully respond with thank you, I heard another voice in a high-pitched tone say, "You're the new principal?" At this point, the secretary stepped away to call Mr. James.

I looked to my left at the woman who entered the office and replied, "Yes."

"I need to talk to you. What they're doing around here ain't right. They just letting people go and making them re-apply for their jobs." Immediately, I knew the school had been reconstituted. This nuanced term referred to schools that were underperforming and taken over by a district, causing employees to re-apply for their positions. It was a legal way to replace staff that was not performing.

Before I could respond, the secretary chimed in, "This is her first day here, she doesn't know everything that's going on!"

"I just need her to know that what they're doing is wrong!"

"What did you do here?"

"I was one of the custodians."

"Well, I am more than happy to find out what happened."

Again she turned to me and said, "If you want to know what's really going on here, meet me at the Giant today at 3:00 up the street, and I'll tell you everything!" In my mind, I thought this lady is crazy. I'm not meeting her at Giant! I was about to respond when a voice came from behind me, "Hello." As I said hello. I heard the custodian mutter, "He's the main one." He quickly ushered me out of the office.

"Don't mind her. She's upset because we had to let her go. She wasn't doing her job as a custodian and was very unreliable."

"Okay. She invited me to Giant at 3:00 pm to discuss what's really happening here at the school."

"Don't mind her; she's just upset."

"Would you like to take a tour of the building?" As we toured the building of cluttered mess, I was struck by the size.

"How many students did you have here last year?"

"About 350."

"That's all?"

"This building is huge for such a small amount of students."

"Yeah. This building used to have a large student population, but over the years, with charter schools on the rise, numbers have dropped." I have always been pro-charter schools, but never really comprehended the hit that public schools took as parents chose to move their students out.

It was clear that the building needed improvements. The dimly lit halls could not cover up the areas that had aged over time and were in disrepair. It seemed that just as the student enrollment declined, so did the building. We walked up what seemed to be a mountain of steps to get to the top floor. I gasped when we reached our destination, both at the climb and the conditions of the floor. It was awful! I guess he saw the look of shock and horror on my face.

"We'll only be using this floor temporarily to serve students as they finish renovating downstairs."

"It may only be used temporarily, but I need them to fix it up! It's awful!" The words came out of my mouth before I could completely filter a better-sounding response. I am a strong believer that school buildings need to possess a vibrant and welcoming environment to serve students so they can achieve. There is an unwanted interaction that occurs when schools fail to provide spaces that are uplifting and modern. I was well aware of the negative influence this type of setting could have on the student body. They would not respect an environment that clearly didn't respect them. I was determined to make sure that my staff and students would experience teaching and learning in an atmosphere that respected them.

The work at my new school was exciting and hard. There were so many things to do, and it felt like they needed to be done yesterday! There was distrust in the school community. They had seen several leadership changes over the last few years and confidence waned. Many people, including those who initially worked closely with me, didn't think I would last. I heard the whispers and knew the gossip of private conversations that often came my way without inquiry. The funny thing was that there was also disbelief of the school's possible success with people I encountered in district meetings. I remember sitting at my first Principal's meeting and being asked by colleagues about the school I had taken over. The reaction was always one of surprise, followed by an expression of hopelessness, "That's a tough school." It was like my first day stepping into the classroom all over again with all the numerous pieces of advice of being stern, not smiling and never turning your back on a student. However, these people didn't know me. They didn't understand that I was born with purpose and perseverance for such a time as this. I was determined to lay a foundation that ensured respect, but offered hope and success.

That first year, I would go in early and leave late, and many times even work on the weekends. There were student fights, faculty disagreements, parental concerns, homeless families and community drama that spilled into the school, all for the principal to fix. It seemed as if drama and trauma infiltrated the building. This was where the work started. Don't be fooled, while academics were important, it all started with creating a positive school culture. My team and I worked tirelessly to address the needs of all these stakeholders and some days were better than others. However, one day as I walked around the school there appeared to be a shift in the environment. Students were in their uniforms, and not blatantly cutting class as they embraced teaching and learning. By no means had things completely changed, but I began to notice a difference. That year the reading and math scores had increased by 15–20%. The largest increase the school had seen in years. While I was excited about the movement, on the inside my mind still struggled with the fact that their scores were still not comparable to other students their age.

Over the next few years as students moved on to high school, staff changed and demands increased for schools, I found myself struggling physically with my health. However, I was always afraid to be out on leave for an extended time because of school so I pushed off surgery until there was a good time. Unfortunately, I never found a good time to be out. I had new Assistant Principals and we were struggling to fill teacher vacancies. Additionally, we had educators who were out due to long-term illnesses. As a result, the school had once again hit some bumps in the roads. I also had a new supervisor who gave limited support, but was quite generous with pointing out any errors. It was the first time in 23 years as an educator, I had a poor evaluation. Looking back now, I recognize that my spirit had been broken that day. I felt stretched and stumped all at the same time, not sure how to proceed.

One day while sitting in a Principal's meeting, I received an email from my supervisor asking me to meet with him. At the end of the meeting, he asked me to follow him to another office. We entered a faintly lit office that was bare and felt slightly frigid. As he sat down across from me, he began, "After careful consideration, we have decided not to bring you back next year as principal." As he continued, I could not make out the hollow echoes of his words.

I just kept replaying his initial words. At some point in the meeting, I realized he had stopped speaking and I was jarred by the silence. I gathered my thoughts and only had the courage to utter one thing, "Is that all?" I said.

"Yes."

"Thank you." I quickly walked out of the building, negating plans with friends and got in my car to race home. My cry on the way home was deep and guttural but could not actually express the depths of heartbreak I was feeling. Words like failure and ineptness were on repeat in my mind. "How do I face my girls?" I thought. I knew they would never judge me, but forming the words to tell them would be hard.

I slowly sunk into a depression. However, each day I reported to school and managed the daily tasks. I met with teachers, parents, students, and community members and prepared the budget and staffing for the upcoming year. I noticed my supervisor coming around having hushed conversations with staff members, and it made me feel so uncomfortable. I smiled as people talked about the things we were going to do in the upcoming year. They didn't have a clue that these things would be done without me. I was operating on autopilot. One afternoon while sitting in my office, I began to experience very sharp abdominal pains. I managed to call a doctor and got an appointment for the next day. The prognosis was as I expected, surgery. Only this time, I didn't have the luxury of putting it off anymore. As I prepared for one surgery, the results came back for another set of tests that detected a tumor in my left ear. This, too, would also need to be removed.

Once again, life had thrown me some curveballs. I lost my job and endured two different surgeries in a span of two months. I had no idea how we were going to survive financially. The darkness of depression took me down a hole I did not want to reside. The fragile nature of my mind sought release and relief, but each day I found it hard to come by. I reached out to different people to pursue leads and find out about jobs. However, with each rejection or dead end, my hope continued to dwindle. One day while searching through my email, I noticed a message from someone I knew who shared information with me about coaching. A person she knew was looking to work with client's pro-bono as a part of her certification. I didn't know what to expect but called the number anyway. It was the best call I ever made. Just like Humpty-Dumpty, she helped me put my life back together again.

DISMISSAL

ESSENTIAL QUESTION: *How do we create spaces for social emotional wellness that addresses the needs of educators?*

All these years later, I can see that five-year-old girl crouching in the bathroom corner of her house, yearning for peace to make itself available in her head. Her little fingers tracing along the outlines of the black and white cold porcelain floor, looking for answers to the questions she didn't know how to ask. Instead, she spent time coloring her mind with a make-believe world full of cautious tales and happy endings. She languished in self-created vivid and verbal stories spoken aloud in spaces no one could hear to ease the pain and discomfort she so often felt. As time went on, the independent self-imposed conversations would grow and take their rightful place to combat the anxiety and loneliness that would sometimes fill her soul. It was in these spaces that she would talk herself to safety. It was in this small compartment of her mind did things become good again.

At fifty, my five-year-old self was still alive and well. She was still trying to skirt the pains of the past and suppress them from taking their place in the present. However, the hunger pains of the past don't disappear just because you "will" them to be gone. The emptiness that comes from not feeding your mind with truth only leaves one's soul growling for peace. As the light-headed feelings of depression begin to take root, the fight for an increased appetite for self-discovery and healing must erode the excessive emotions encountered. This is the disruption I had been seeking all my life.

I jumped into the car that day, full of anxiety and apprehension. The drive into Washington DC wasn't long. However, in my head, I took a long journey of possible outcomes. Would we connect? Would coaching work any better than therapy? How much of my life was she expecting me to share? The list of questions and thoughts continued to play throughout my head. I pulled into the neighborhood and immediately noticed the stillness. The street was scantily scattered with people. I entered the building and felt its history. The foyer was spacious and dimly lit. It felt as if the building had been "grandfathered" into what seemed like the modern and contemporary movement of new housing plaguing countless DC streets. As we sat down to talk, I immediately felt a sense of calm. It was her voice. The tone was soothing and nurturing. My posture and mind began to embrace relaxation. We recounted my struggles and history. I once again fell into a flurry of tears. The well of feelings had been pent up for so long that my tears found a comfortable place in the conversation each time I spoke of it. Each word and tear allowed me to be in my most authentic state. It was raw, revealing and challenged me to sit in the reality of my life. No more running. No more ignoring, No more muting. No more excuses!

Each week I stood in my naked truth and began to challenge the rise of emotions that often came up that kept me stuck. In these moments, I struggled with provoking thoughts, questions, and realizations. Educators who want to make a difference go to work each day, hoping to impact the lives of their students and staff. Some would argue that with impact comes connection. Sometimes that connection comes with a weight that unexpectedly influences our personal lives in real and meaningful ways. It disrupts the theories taught in college classrooms and brings you face-to-face with the humanity of this calling. It corrals in school buildings, strolls hallways, sits in offices, and stands in classrooms. The educator's journey goes beyond his/her students and parents; it is a compilation of pains never healed, truths never told, and mental health support not yet tapped.

I was finally doing the work and my coach kept encouraging me to dig deep and release. She spent weeks trying to persuade me to visit the Cathedral in DC. She felt that it would offer me a sense of grace and peace. I had never been there and didn't know what to expect. Finally, one Sunday after church, my youngest daughter and I journeyed to see the Washington National Cathedral. We turned onto the street when

My youngest daughter exclaimed, "Mommy are we going to church again?"

I chuckled, "Sort of."

"Why are we going to church twice?" she questioned.

"We are not going to a church service. We are just going to walk around."

"Huh? I don't understand."

"You will," I replied. We got out of the car and began to make our way amidst the other visitors. It was a beautiful day, and I decided to walk in the garden first. I was captivated by the greenery and cultivated flowers. It was beautiful.

"Mommy, this is pretty," she yelled as we approached the Gazebo.

The landscape and carefully designed paths echoed inspiration with each step and turn. I began to take pictures to capture the scenery, but more importantly, to seize this single moment between a mother and daughter. It was everything as I listened to her faint chatter amongst the serenity that occupied every part of the garden and overpowered the thick city air. Beyond the garden, we excitedly made our way inside the Cathedral. She was filled with a hundred questions and comments.

"Mommy, this place is big. Look at the pictures. What kind of music is that? Why are people lighting candles?" As we sat, I guided her to sit in silence and focus on all the things she heard and saw for us to talk about later. I sat in silence to create a shift from speaking to feeling. I wanted to welcome the grace that God was offering to me. Before I knew it, my head was bowed in prayer and meditation. I was once again releasing and championing a new beginning. With raised head and opened hands, I offered myself compassion and moved through the process of RAIN.

✳ ✳ ✳ ✳ ✳

1. **R**ecognize what is going on

2. **A**llow the experience to be there

3. **I**nvestigate it with kindness

4. **N**atural awareness comes from not identifying with the experience but the compassion you have for yourself

My journey in education has allowed me to flourish in chaos and celebrate a culture that cultivates community in many beautiful and unique ways. I've held many positions, and each time, I exceeded the emotional and social expectations created in unrealistic constructs beyond the school walls. However, there is a price to pay with this responsibility. My growth and evolution have been 25 years in the making, and today I recognize how the experiences of adversity and chronic stress, both personally and professionally, connected me to a dysfunction that failed to provide a safe space for recovery. It almost killed me. The State of Education must create and implement systemic guidance that promotes adult social and emotional wellness and leads to effective organizational change. That day at the Cathedral changed my life.

It was in this place that I decided to no longer shift in the shadows of my mind. This is not where I wanted to die. Instead, I held on to the words of my coach, "Find your voice again and connect more deeply with your soul and others, in order to mobilize your great courage and innate creativity in service of yourself, your family and the world." This was my gift created by God to give to the world.